BILLY GRAHAM

Evangelistic Association

Always Good News.

Dear Friend,

I am pleased to send you this copy of *The Power of the Blood of Christ* by Andrew Murray. My mother loved to read Murray's books, which were always filled with great insights from God's Word.

I believe you'll be edified and encouraged by this book, which focuses on the significance of the blood Jesus shed on Calvary. Learning about its power— in waging spiritual warfare against our enemy and in coping with difficult situations—means greater peace and security in all areas of our lives. Murray helps us understand, in a practical way, how to overcome the evil one "*by the blood of the Lamb and by the word of [our] testimony*" (Revelation 12:11, NIV). I pray you'll be blessed as you discover this secret to victorious Christian living.

For nearly 60 years the Billy Graham Evangelistic Association has worked to take the Good News of Jesus Christ throughout the world by every effective means available, and I'm excited about what God will do in the years ahead.

We would appreciate knowing how our ministry has touched your life. May God richly bless you.

Sincerely,

Franklin Graham
President

D1024305

If you would like to know more about our ministry, please contact us:

In the U.S.:

Billy Graham Evangelistic Association
1 Billy Graham Parkway
Charlotte, NC 28201-0001
billygraham.org
info@bgea.org
Toll-free: 1-877-2GRAHAM (1-877-247-2426)

In Canada:

Billy Graham Evangelistic Association of Canada
20 Hopewell Way NE
Calgary, AB T3J 5H5
billygraham.ca
Toll-free: 1-888-393-0003

THE POWER OF THE BLOOD OF *Christ*

ANDREW MURRAY

This *Billy Graham Library Selection* is published for
the Billy Graham Evangelistic Association
by Whitaker House.

WHITAKER
HOUSE

A *Billy Graham Library Selection* designates materials that are appropriate for a well-rounded collection of quality Christian literature, including both classic and contemporary reading and reference materials.

Publisher's note:

The author's selection of Bible versions has been retained whenever possible, including the Revised Version when it was originally cited. The text of this book, however, has been updated for the modern reader. Words, expressions, and sentence structure have been revised for clarity and readability.

Unless otherwise indicated, all Scripture quotations are taken from the King James Version (KJV) of the Holy Bible. Scripture quotations marked (RV) are taken from the Revised Version of the Holy Bible.

THE POWER OF THE BLOOD OF CHRIST

(Previously published as *The Power of the Blood of Jesus*)

ISBN-978-1-60374-238-2
Previous ISBN-13: 978-0-88368-242-5
Printed in the United States of America
©1993 by Whitaker House

WHITAKER
HOUSE

1030 Hunt Valley Circle
New Kensington, PA 15068
whitakerhouse.com

Contents

Preface 7

1. What the Scriptures Teach
    about the Blood 9

2. Redemption by Blood 25

3. Reconciliation through the Blood 39

4. Cleansing through the Blood 53

5. Sanctification through the Blood 67

6. Cleansed by the Blood to
    Serve the Living God 83

7. Dwelling in *"The Holiest"*
    through the Blood 99

8. Life in the Blood 121

9. Victory through the Blood 135

10. Heavenly Joy through the Blood 151

About the Author 167

Note by Translator

It is necessary to remember that, throughout these chapters, Dr. Murray refers only to "sacrificial blood." The blood in the Bible is always that.

It should be noted when reading chapter three that, in the Dutch Bible that Dr. Murray used, the word *verzoening* is used for "propitiation." *Verzoening* means "reconciliation," and that is the word used in this translation.

Preface

Preface

This book is a translation of a portion of a series of addresses by my late father, the Reverend Andrew Murray, M.A., D.D., on "The Power of the Blood of Jesus."

The translator is the Reverend William M. Douglas, B.A., who for many years was my father's close friend, having been associated with him in connection with the South African Keswick Convention Movement. During my father's lifetime, he permitted Mr. Douglas to translate his book, *The Prayer Life,* and he became the biographer of my father after his death.

I have read the manuscript and think the translation is excellent. He has reproduced the thoughts of my father exactly.

I feel sure that much blessing will result from the prayerful and thoughtful reading of these chapters.

Trusting you may learn to value and to live in the experience of the power of the precious blood of our Lord and Savior Jesus Christ.

I remain,
Yours in the blessed Master's service,
—M. E. MURRAY

one
What the Scriptures
Teach about the Blood

What the Scriptures Teach about the Blood

Not without blood.
—Hebrews 9:7

God has spoken to us in the Scriptures in many differ-ent portions and in various manners, but the voice is always the same. It is always the Word of the same God.

Hence, we see the importance of treating the Bible as a whole and receiving the witness it gives in its vari-ous portions concerning certain definite truths. In this way, we learn to recognize the place these truths actu-ally occupy in revelation, or rather, in the heart of God. Also, in this way, we begin to discover which foundational truths of the Bible demand our attention above all others. Standing so prominently as they do in each new depar-ture in God's revelation, remaining unchanged when the dispensation changes, they carry a divine indication of their importance.

It is my objective, in the chapters that follow this intro-ductory one, to show what the Scriptures teach us con-cerning the glorious power of the blood of Jesus and the wonderful blessings procured for us by it. I cannot lay a better foundation for my exposition, nor give a better proof of the superlative glory of that blood as the power of redemption, than by asking my readers to follow me through the Bible and thus see the unique place that is given to the blood from the beginning to the end of God's revelation of Himself to man, as recorded in the Bible.

It will become clear that there is no single scriptural idea, from Genesis to Revelation, more constantly and more prominently kept in view than that expressed by the words *the blood.* Our inquiry, therefore, is what the Scriptures teach us about the blood:

- First, in the Old Testament
- Second, in the teaching of our Lord Jesus Himself
- Third, in what the apostles taught
- Fourth, in what John told us of the blood in Revelation
- Last, in the lessons we can learn about the blood from Scripture

What the Old Testament Teaches

The scriptural record about the blood begins at the gates of Eden. I do not enter into the unrevealed mysteries of Eden, but in connection with the sacrifice of Abel, all is plain. He brought *"the firstlings of his flock"* (Genesis 4:4) to the Lord as a sacrifice, and there, in connection with the first act of worship recorded in the Bible, blood was shed. We learn from Hebrews 11:4 that it was *"by faith"* that Abel offered an acceptable sacrifice, and his name stands first in the record of those whom the Bible calls *believers.* He had this witness given to him, *"that he was righteous"* (Hebrews 11:4). His faith, and God's good pleasure in him, are closely connected with the sacrificial blood.

In light of later revelation, this testimony, given at the very beginning of human history, is of deep significance. It shows that there can be no approach to God, no fellowship with Him by faith, no enjoyment of His favor, apart from the blood.

The new earth had to be baptized with blood.

Scripture gives only a brief account of the following sixteen centuries. Then came the flood, which was God's judgment on sin, by the destruction of the world of mankind. But God brought forth a new earth from that awful baptism of water.

Notice, however, that the new earth also had to be baptized with blood, and the first recorded act of Noah, after he had left the ark, was the offering of a burnt sacrifice to God. As it was with Abel, so was it with Noah at a new beginning; it was *"not without blood."*

Sin once again prevailed, and God laid an entirely new foundation for the establishment of His kingdom on earth.

By the divine call of Abraham and the miraculous birth of Isaac, God undertook the formation of a people to serve Him. But this purpose was not accomplished apart from the shedding of the blood. This is apparent in the most solemn hour of Abraham's life.

What the Scriptures Teach about the Blood

God had already entered into covenant relationship with Abraham, and his faith had already been severely tried and had stood the test. It was reckoned, or counted to him, for righteousness (Romans 4:9). Yet he had to learn that Isaac, the son of promise, who belonged wholly to God, could be truly surrendered to God only by death. Isaac had to die. For Abraham, as well as for Isaac, only by death could freedom from the self-life be obtained.

Abraham had to offer Isaac on the altar. (See Genesis 22:1–18.) This was not an arbitrary command of God. It was the revelation of a divine truth, that only through death is it possible for a life to be truly consecrated to God. But it was impossible for Isaac to die and rise again from the dead, for on account of sin, death would hold him fast. But the Scriptures tell us that Isaac's life was spared, and a ram was offered in his place (verse 13). Through the blood that then flowed on Mount Moriah, his life was spared. He and the people who sprang from him lived before God *"not without blood."* By that blood, however, he was, in a sense, raised again from the dead. The great lesson of substitution is taught clearly here.

Four hundred years passed, and Isaac became, in Egypt, the people of Israel. Through her deliverance from Egyptian bondage, Israel was to be recognized as God's firstborn among the nations. Here, also, it was *"not without blood."* Neither the electing grace of God, nor His covenant with Abraham, nor the exercise of His omnipotence, which could so easily have destroyed their oppressors, could dispense with the necessity of the blood.

What the blood accomplished on Mount Moriah for one person, who was the father of the nation, now had to be experienced by that nation. By the sprinkling of the door frames of the Israelites with the blood of the Paschal lamb, and by the institution of the Passover as an enduring ordinance with the words, *"When I see the blood, I will pass over you"* (Exodus 12:13), the people were taught that life can be obtained only by the death of a substitute. Life was possible for them only through the blood of a life given in their place, and this life could be taken hold of by the sprinkling of that blood.

Fifty days later, this lesson was enforced in a striking manner. Israel had reached Sinai. God had given His law as the foundation of His covenant. That covenant now had to be established, but as it is expressly stated in Hebrews 9:7, *"not without blood."* The sacrificial blood had to be sprinkled, first on the altar; then on the book of the covenant, representing God's side of that covenant; then on the people, with the declaration, *"Behold the blood of the covenant"* (Exodus 24:8).

In that blood, the covenant had its foundation and power. It is by the blood alone that God and man can be brought into covenant fellowship. That which had been foreshadowed at the gate of Eden, on Mount Ararat, on Moriah, and in Egypt was now confirmed at the foot of Sinai in a most solemn manner. Without blood there could be no access by sinful man to a holy God.

There is, however, a significant difference between the manner of applying the blood in the former cases as compared with the latter. On Moriah the life was redeemed by the shedding of the blood. In Egypt it was sprinkled on the doorposts of the houses; but at Sinai, it was sprinkled on the persons themselves. The contact was closer, the application more powerful.

What the Scriptures Teach about the Blood

Immediately after the establishment of the covenant, the command was given, *"Let them make me a sanctuary; that I may dwell among them"* (Exod. 25:8). They were to enjoy the full blessedness of having the God of the covenant abiding among them. Through His grace, they could find Him and serve Him in His house.

Nothing can dispense with the necessity of the blood.

He Himself gave, with the minutest care, directions for the arrangement and service of that house. But you will notice that the blood is the center and reason of all this. Draw near to the vestibule of the earthly temple of the heavenly King, and the first thing visible is the altar of burnt offering, where the sprinkling of blood continues, without ceasing, from morning until evening. Enter the Holy Place, and the most conspicuous thing is the golden altar of incense, which also, together with the veil, is constantly sprinkled with the blood. Ask what lies beyond the Holy Place, and you will be told that it is the Most Holy Place where God dwells. If you ask how He dwells there and how He is approached, you will be told *"not without blood."* The golden throne, where His glory shines, is itself sprinkled with the blood once every year when the high priest alone enters to bring in the blood and to worship God. The highest act in that worship is the sprinkling of the blood.

If you inquire further, you will be told that, for everything, the blood is always the one necessary thing. At the consecration of the house or of the priests, at the birth of a child, in the deepest penitence on account of sin, in the highest festival—always and in everything—the way to fellowship with God is through the blood alone.

This continued for fifteen hundred years. At Sinai, in the desert, at Shiloh, in the temple on Mount Moriah, it continued—until our Lord came to make an end of all shadows by bringing in the substance and by establishing a fellowship with the Holy One, in spirit and truth.

What Our Lord Jesus Himself Taught about the Blood

With the coming of Christ, old things passed away and all things became new (2 Corinthians 5:17). He came from the Father in heaven, and He told us the way to the Father in divine words.

It is sometimes said that the words *"not without blood"* belong to the Old Testament. But what did our Lord Jesus Christ say? Notice, first, that when John the Baptist announced His coming, he spoke of Him as filling a dual office: as *"the Lamb of God, which taketh away the sin of the world"* (John 1:29), and then as *"He which baptizeth with the Holy Ghost"* (verse 33). The outpouring of the blood of the Lamb of God had to take place before the outpouring of the Spirit could be bestowed. Only when all that the Old Testament taught about the blood had been fulfilled could the dispensation of the Spirit begin.

The Lord Jesus Christ Himself plainly declared that His death on the cross was the purpose for which He came into the world, that it was the necessary condition for the redemption and life that He came to bring. He clearly stated that, in connection with His death, the shedding of His blood was necessary.

What the Scriptures Teach about the Blood

In the synagogue at Capernaum, He spoke of Himself as the *"bread of life"* (John 6:35, 48); of His flesh, He said that He would *"give* [it] *for the life of the world"* (verse 51). Four times over He said most emphatically, *"Except ye... drink* [my] *blood, ye have no life in you. Whoso...drinketh my blood, hath eternal life....my blood is drink indeed. He that...drinketh my blood dwelleth in me, and I in him"* (verses 53–56). Our Lord thus declared the fundamental fact that He Himself, as the Son of the Father, who came to restore to us our lost life, could do this in no other way than by dying for us, by shedding His blood for us, and then by making us partakers of its power.

Our Lord confirmed the teaching of the Old Testament offerings—that man can live only through the death of another and thus obtain a life that, through resurrection, has become eternal.

But Christ Himself cannot make us partakers of the eternal life that He has procured for us except by the shedding of His blood and by causing us to drink it. Marvelous fact! *"Not without blood"* can eternal life be ours.

Equally striking is our Lord's declaration of the same truth on the last night of His earthly life. Before He completed the great work of His life by giving it as *"a ransom for many"* (Matthew 20:28), He instituted the Holy Supper, saying, *"Drink ye all of it; for this is my blood of the new testament, which is shed for many for the remission of sins"* (Matthew 26:27–28). *"Without shedding of blood is no remission* [of sins]" (Hebrews 9:22). Without remission of sins, there is no life. But by the shedding of His blood, He has obtained a new life for us. By what He calls "the drinking of His blood," He shares His life with us. The blood shed in the atonement—which frees us from the guilt of sin and from death, the punishment of sin—the blood, which we drink by faith, bestows His life on us.

The Teaching of the Apostles under the Inspiration of the Holy Spirit

After His resurrection and ascension, our Lord was no longer known by the apostles *"after the flesh"* (2 Corinthians 5:16). All that was symbolic had passed away, and the deep spiritual truths expressed symbolically were unveiled.

But there is no veiling of the blood. It still occupies a prominent place.

Turn first to the epistle to the Hebrews, which was written purposely to show that the temple service had become unprofitable and was intended by God to pass away, now that Christ had come.

Here, if anywhere, it might be expected that the Holy Spirit would emphasize the true spirituality of God's purpose, yet it is just here that the blood of Jesus is spoken of in a manner that imparts a new value to the phrase.

Concerning our Lord, we read that *"by his own blood he entered in once into the holy place"* (Hebrews 9:12). *"The blood of Christ...*[will] *purge your conscience"* (verse 14). *"Having therefore, brethren, boldness to enter into the holiest by the blood of Jesus"* (Hebrews 10:19). *"Ye are come...to Jesus the mediator of the new covenant, and to the blood of sprinkling"* (Hebrews 12:22, 24). *"Jesus also, that he might sanctify the people with his own blood, suffered without the gate"* (Hebrews 13:12). *"God...brought again from the dead our Lord Jesus, that great shepherd of the sheep, through the blood of the everlasting covenant"* (verse 20).

By such words, the Holy Spirit teaches us that the blood is really the central power of our entire redemption. *"Not without blood"* is as valid in the New Testament as in the Old.

The blood still occupies a prominent place.

Nothing but the blood of Jesus, shed in His death for sin, can cover sin on God's side or remove it on ours.

We find the same teaching in the writings of the apostles. Paul wrote of *"being justified freely by his grace through the redemption that is in Christ Jesus...through faith in his blood"* (Romans 3:24–25), and of *"being now justified by his blood"* (Romans 5:9).

To the Corinthians, he declared that the *"cup of blessing which we bless, is...the communion of the blood of Christ"* (1 Corinthians 10:16).

In the epistle to the Galatians, he used the word *cross* to convey the same meaning (see, for example, Galatians 6:14), while in Colossians he united the two words and spoke of *"the blood of his cross"* (Colossians 1:20).

He reminded the Ephesians that *"we have redemption through his blood"* (Ephesians 1:7) and that we *"are made nigh by the blood of Christ"* (Ephesians 2:13).

Peter reminded his readers that they were *"elect... unto obedience and sprinkling of the blood of Jesus Christ* (1 Peter 1:2), that they were redeemed by *"the precious blood of Christ"* (verse 19).

The Power of the Blood of Christ

See how John assured his *"little children"* (1 John 2:1) that *"the blood of Jesus Christ His Son cleanseth us from all sin"* (1 John 1:7). The Son is He *"that came...not by water only, but by water and blood"* (1 John 5:6).

All of these writers agreed together in mentioning the blood and in glorying in it as the power by which eternal redemption through Christ is fully accomplished and is then applied by the Holy Spirit.

But perhaps this is merely earthly language. What does heaven have to say? Let us examine the book of Revelation.

What the Book of Revelation Says concerning the Blood

It is of the greatest importance to notice that, in the revelation that God has given in this book of the glory of His throne and the blessedness of those who surround it, the blood still retains its remarkably prominent place.

On the throne John saw *"a Lamb as it had been slain"* (Revelation 5:6). As the elders fell down before the Lamb, they sang a new song, saying, *"Thou art worthy...for thou wast slain, and hast redeemed us to God by thy blood"* (verse 9).

Later on, when he saw the great company that no man could number, he was told in reply to his question as to who they were, "[They have] *washed their robes, and made them white in the blood of the Lamb"* (Revelation 7:14).

Then again, when he heard the song of victory over the defeat of Satan, its words were, *"They overcame him by the blood of the Lamb"* (Revelation 12:11).

What the Scriptures Teach about the Blood

In the glory of heaven, as seen by John, there was no phrase by which the great purposes of God, the wondrous love of the Son of God, the power of His redemption, and the joy and thanksgiving of the redeemed could be gathered up and expressed besides this: *"The blood of the Lamb"* (Revelation 12:11).

Lessons to Learn from the Scriptures

From the beginning to the end of Scripture, from the closing of the gates of Eden to the opening of the gates of the heavenly Zion, there runs through Scripture a golden thread. It is the blood that unites the beginning and the end, that gloriously restores what sin had destroyed.

It is not difficult to see what lessons the Lord wishes us to learn from the fact that the blood occupies such a prominent place in Scripture.

The Only Means of Dealing with Sin

God has no other way of dealing with sin, or the sinner, except through the blood. For victory over sin and the deliverance of the sinner, God has no other means or thought than *"the blood of Christ"* (1 Corinthians 10:16). Yes, it is indeed something that surpasses all understanding.

All the wonders of grace are focused here: the incarnation, by which He took upon Himself our flesh and blood; the love, which did not spare itself but surrendered itself to death; the righteousness, which could not forgive sin until the penalty was borne; the substitution, by which He, the Righteous One, atoned for us, the unrighteous; the atonement for sin; and the justification of the sinner. In this way, renewed fellowship with God was made possible, together with the cleansing and sanctification to equip us for the enjoyment of that fellowship; the true oneness in life with the Lord Jesus, as He gives us His blood to drink; the eternal joy of the hymn of praise, *"Thou...hast redeemed us to God"* (Revelation 5:9). All these are but rays of the wondrous light that are reflected upon us from *"the precious blood of Christ"* (1 Peter 1:19).

The Right View of the Blood

The blood must have the same place in our hearts that it has with God. From the beginning of God's dealings with man, yes, from before the foundation of the world, the heart of God has rejoiced in that blood. Our hearts will never rest, nor find salvation, until we, too, learn to walk and glory in the power of that blood.

It is not only the penitent sinner, longing for pardon, who must thus value it. No! The redeemed will see that just as God in His temple sits upon a throne of grace, where the blood is ever in evidence, so there is nothing that draws our hearts nearer to God, filling them with God's love, joy, and glory, as living in a constant, spiritual view of that blood.

The Blessing and Power of the Blood

Let us take time and trouble to learn the full blessing and power of that blood. The blood of Jesus is the greatest mystery of eternity, the deepest mystery of divine wisdom. Let us not imagine that we can easily grasp its meaning. God thought four thousand years were necessary to prepare men for it, and we also must take time if we are to gain a knowledge of the power of the blood.

Even taking time is of no avail unless there is also the effort of making a sacrifice. Sacrificial blood always meant the offering of a life. The Israelite could not obtain blood for the pardon of his sin unless the life of something that belonged to him was offered in sacrifice. The Lord Jesus did not offer up His own life and shed His blood in order to spare us from the sacrifice of our lives. No, indeed! Rather, He did so to make the sacrifice of our lives possible and desirable.

The hidden value of His blood is the spirit of self-sacrifice.

The hidden value of His blood is the spirit of self-sacrifice, and where the blood really touches the heart, it works out in that heart a similar spirit of self-sacrifice. We learn to give up ourselves and our lives, in order to press into the full power of that new life that the blood has provided.

We give our time so that we may become acquainted with these things by God's Word. We separate ourselves from sin, worldly mindedness, and self-will so that the power of the blood may not be hindered, for it is just these things that the blood seeks to remove.

We surrender ourselves wholly to God in prayer and faith so as not to think our own thoughts, and not to hold our own lives as a prize, but rather to possess nothing except what He bestows. Then He reveals to us the glorious and blessed life that has been prepared for us by the blood.

The Revelation of the Power of the Blood

We can rely on the Lord Jesus to reveal to us the power of His blood. It is by this confident trust in Him that the blessing obtained by the blood becomes ours. We must never, in thought, separate the blood from the High Priest who shed it and who ever lives to apply it.

He who once gave His blood for us will surely, every moment, impart its effectiveness. Trust Him to do this. Trust Him to open your eyes and to give you a deeper spiritual insight. Trust Him to teach you to think about the blood as God thinks about it. Trust Him to impart to you, and to make effective in you, all that He enables you to see.

Above all, trust Him in the power of His eternal high priesthood to work out in you, unceasingly, the full merits of His blood so that your whole life may be an uninterrupted abiding in the sanctuary of God's presence.

Believer, you who have come to the knowledge of the precious blood, listen to the invitation of your Lord. Come nearer. Let Him teach you; let Him bless you. Let Him cause His blood to become spirit, life, power, and truth to you.

Begin now, at once, to open your soul in faith, to receive the full, mighty, heavenly effects of the precious blood, in a more glorious manner than you have ever experienced. He Himself will work these things out in your life.

two
Redemption by Blood

t w o

Redemption by Blood

*Ye were not redeemed with corruptible things,...
but with the precious blood of Christ, as of a
lamb without blemish and without spot.*
—1 Peter 1:18–19

The shedding of His blood was the culmination of the sufferings of our Lord. The atonement offered by those sufferings was in that shed blood. It is therefore of great importance that the believer should not rest satisfied with the mere acceptance of the blessed truth that he is redeemed by that blood, but that he should press on to a fuller knowledge of what is meant by that statement and to learn what that blood is intended to do in a surrendered soul.

Its effects are manifold, for we read in Scripture of the following:

- Reconciliation through the blood
- Cleansing through the blood
- Sanctification through the blood
- Union with God through the blood
- Victory over Satan through the blood
- Life through the blood

Redemption by Blood

These are separate blessings but are all included in one phrase: "redemption by the blood." It is only where the believer understands what these blessings are, and by what means they may become his, that he can experience the full power of redemption.

Before considering these blessings in detail, let us first inquire, in a more general way, concerning the power of the blood of Jesus:

- First, where does the power of that blood lie?
- Second, what has that power accomplished?
- Third, how can we experience its effects?

Where Does the Power of the Blood Lie?

What is it that gives such power to the blood of Jesus? How is it that, in the blood alone, there is power possessed by nothing else?

The answer to this question is found in Leviticus 17:11: *"For the life of the flesh is in the blood: and I have given it to you upon the altar to make an atonement for your souls: for it is the blood that maketh an atonement for the soul."*

Because the soul, or life, is in the blood, and because the blood is offered to God on the altar, it has redemptive power.

The Life Is in the Blood

The value of the blood corresponds to the value of the life that is in it. The life of a sheep or goat is of less value than the life of an ox, and so the blood of a sheep or a goat in an offering is of less value than the blood of an ox. (See Leviticus 4:13–14, 27–28.) The life of man is more valuable than that of many sheep or oxen.

The Power of the Blood of Christ

Now, who can tell the value or the power of the blood of Jesus? The soul of the holy Son of God dwelt in that blood. The eternal life of the Godhead was carried in that blood. (See Acts 20:28.)

The power of that blood in its many effects is nothing less than the eternal power of God Himself. What a glorious thought for everyone who desires to experience the full power of the blood!

Offered to God on the Altar

But the power of the blood lies above everything else in the fact that it is offered to God on the altar for redemption. When we think of blood as shed, we think of death; death follows when the blood or the soul is poured out. Death makes us think of sin, for death is the punishment of sin (Romans 6:23). God gave Israel the blood on the altar as the atonement, or covering, for sin. This means that the sins of the transgressor were laid on the victim, and its death was reckoned as the death or punishment for the sins laid upon it.

The blood was thus life given up to death for the satisfaction of the law of God, and in obedience to His command. Sin was so entirely covered and atoned for that it was no longer reckoned as that of the transgressor. The transgressor was forgiven.

But all these sacrifices and offerings were only types and shadows, until the Lord Jesus came. His blood was the reality to which these types pointed.

His blood was in itself of infinite value because it carried His soul, or life. But the atoning virtue of His blood was infinite also, because of the manner in which it was shed.

Redemption by Blood

In holy obedience to the Father's will, He subjected Himself to the penalty of the broken law by pouring out His soul unto death. By that death, not only was the penalty borne but the law was satisfied and the Father was glorified. His blood atoned for sin and thus made it powerless. It has a marvelous power for removing sin and opening heaven for the sinner, whom it cleanses and sanctifies and makes fit for heaven.

In the blood, there is power possessed by nothing else.

It is because of the wonderful Person whose blood was shed, and because of the wonderful way in which it was shed, fulfilling the law of God while satisfying its just demands, that the blood of Jesus has such wonderful power. It is the blood of atonement, and hence it has the power to redeem, accomplishing everything for and in the sinner that is necessary for salvation.

What Has That Power Accomplished?

As we see something of the wonders that this power has accomplished, we will be encouraged to believe that it can do the same for us. Our best plan is to note how the Scriptures glory in the great things that have taken place through the power of the blood of Jesus.

The Blood Opened the Grave

We read in Hebrews 13:20, *"The God of peace...brought again from the dead our Lord Jesus, that great shepherd of the sheep, through the blood of the everlasting covenant."* It was through the virtue of the blood that God raised up

Jesus from the dead. God's almighty power was not exerted, apart from the blood, to raise Jesus from the dead.

He came to earth as the surety and bearer of the sin of mankind. It was through the shedding of His blood alone that He had the right, as man, to rise again and to obtain eternal life through resurrection. His blood had satisfied the law and righteousness of God. By so doing, He had overcome the power of sin and brought it to nothing. In the same way, death was defeated; its sting, sin, had been removed; and the Devil, who had the power of death, was also defeated, having now lost all right over Him and us. His blood has destroyed the power of death, the Devil, and hell; the blood of Jesus has opened the grave.

He who truly believes this perceives the close connection that exists between the blood and the almighty power of God. It is only through the blood that God exerts His almightiness in dealing with sinful men. Where the blood is, there the resurrection power of God gives entrance into eternal life. The blood has made a complete end of all the power of death and hell. Its effects surpass all human thought.

The Blood of Jesus Opened Heaven

We read in Hebrews 9:12 that Christ *"by his own blood... entered in once into the holy place, having obtained eternal redemption for us."*

We know that, in the Old Testament tabernacle, God's manifested presence was inside the veil. No power of man could remove that veil. The high priest alone could enter there, but only with blood or at the loss of his own life. That was a picture of the power of sin in the flesh, which separates us from God. The eternal righteousness of God guarded the entrance to the Most Holy Place so that no flesh might approach Him.

But now our Lord appears, not in an earthly temple, but in the true temple. As High Priest and representative of His people, He asks for Himself, and for the sinful children of Adam, entrance into the presence of the Holy One. *"That where I am, there* [they] *may be also"* (John 14:3) is His request. He asks that heaven may be opened for each one, even for the greatest sinner, who believes in Him. His request is granted. But how is this? It is through the blood. He entered through His own blood. The blood of Jesus has opened heaven.

The blood keeps heaven open for sinners.

So it is always through the blood that the throne of grace remains settled in heaven. Nearest to *"God the Judge of all"* (Hebrews 12:23), and to *"Jesus the mediator"* (verse 24), the Holy Spirit gives a prominent place to *"the blood of sprinkling"* (verse 24).

It is the constant "speaking" of that blood that keeps heaven open for sinners and sends streams of blessing down on earth. It is through that blood that Jesus, as Mediator, carries on His mediatorial work without ceasing. The throne of grace ever owes its existence to the power of that blood.

Oh, the wonderful power of the blood of Christ! Just as it has broken open the gates of the grave and of hell to let Jesus out, and us with Him, so it has opened the gates of heaven for Him, and us with Him, to enter. The blood has an almighty power over the kingdom of darkness and hell beneath, and over the kingdom of heaven and its glory above.

All-Powerful in the Human Heart

Since the blood avails so powerfully with God and over Satan, does it not avail even more powerfully with man, for whose sake it was actually shed? We may be sure of it.

The wonderful power of the blood is especially manifested on behalf of sinners on earth. Our text is just one of many Scripture passages where this is emphasized. *"Ye were...redeemed...from your vain conversation...with the precious blood of Christ"* (1 Peter 1:18–19).

The word *"redeemed"* has a depth of meaning. It particularly indicates deliverance from slavery by emancipation or purchase. The sinner is enslaved under the hostile power of Satan, the curse of the law, and sin. Now it is proclaimed, "You are redeemed through the blood," which had paid the debt of guilt and destroyed the power of Satan, the curse, and sin.

Where this proclamation is heard and received, redemption begins in a true deliverance from a vain manner of life, from a life of sin. The word *redemption* includes everything God does for a sinner from the pardon of sin, in which it begins (Ephesians 1:14; 4:30), to the full deliverance of the body by resurrection (Romans 8:23–24).

Those to whom Peter wrote were *"elect...unto...sprinkling of the blood of Jesus Christ"* (1 Peter 1:2). The proclamation about the precious blood had touched their hearts and brought them to repentance, awakening faith in them, and filling their souls with life and joy. Each believer was an illustration of the wonderful power of the blood.

Further on, when Peter exhorted them to holiness, his plea was still the precious blood. He wanted them to focus on it.

Redemption begins in a true deliverance from a life of sin.

For the Jew as well as the Gentile, there was only one means of deliverance from the power of sin. It is still the one power that brings about daily deliverance for sinners. How could it be otherwise? The blood that availed so powerfully in heaven and over hell is all-powerful in a sinner's heart, too. It is impossible for us to think too highly of, or to expect too much from, the power of Jesus' blood.

How Does This Power Work?

Our third question is this: In what conditions, or under what circumstances, can the power of the blood secure, unhindered in us, the mighty results it is intended to produce?

Through Faith

The first answer, just as it is everywhere in the kingdom of God, is that it is through faith. But faith is largely dependent on knowledge. If knowledge of what the blood can accomplish is imperfect, then faith expects little, and the more powerful effects of the blood are impossible. Many Christians think that if they have received assurance of the pardon of their sins through faith in the blood, then they have a sufficient knowledge of its effects.

They have no idea that the words of God, like God Himself, are inexhaustible, that they have a wealth of meaning and blessing that surpasses all understanding.

They do not remember that, when the Holy Spirit speaks of cleansing through the blood, such words are only imperfect human expressions of the effects and experiences by which the blood, in an unspeakably glorious manner, will reveal its heavenly life-giving power to the soul. Feeble ideas of its power prevent the deeper and more perfect manifestations of its effects.

As we seek to find out what the Scriptures teach about the blood, we will see that faith in the blood, even as we now understand it, can produce greater results in us than we have yet known; and in the future, a ceaseless blessing may be ours.

Our faith may be strengthened by noticing what the blood has already accomplished. Heaven and hell bear witness to this. Faith will grow by exercising confidence in the fathomless fullness of the promises of God. Let us heartily expect that, as we enter more deeply into the fountain of Christ's blood, its cleansing, quickening, life-giving power will be revealed more blessedly.

When we bathe, we enter into the most intimate relationship with the water, giving ourselves up to its cleansing effects. The blood of Jesus is described as *"a fountain opened...for sin and for uncleanness"* (Zechariah 13:1). By the power of the Holy Spirit, it streams through the heavenly temple. By faith, I place myself in closest contact with this heavenly stream; I yield myself to it; I let it cover me and go through me. I bathe in the fountain. It cannot withhold its cleansing and strengthening power. I must, in simple faith, turn away from what is seen, to plunge into the spiritual fountain that represents the Savior's blood, with the assurance that it will manifest its blessed power in me.

So let us, with childlike, persevering, and expectant faith, open our souls to an ever increasing experience of the wonderful power of the blood.

The Spirit and the Blood

But there is still another reply to the question as to what else is necessary so that the blood may manifest its power. Scripture connects the blood most closely with the Spirit. It is only where the Spirit works that the power of the blood will be manifested.

Faith in the blood produces great results.

We read in 1 John that *"there are three that bear witness in earth, the Spirit, and the water, and the blood: and these three agree in one"* (1 John 5:8). The water refers to baptism unto repentance and the laying aside of sin. The blood refers to redemption in Christ. The Spirit is He who supplies power to the water and the blood. So also, the Spirit and the blood are associated in Hebrews 9:14, where we read, *"How much more shall the blood of Christ, who through the eternal Spirit offered himself without spot to God, purge your conscience."* It was by the eternal Spirit in our Lord that His blood had its value and power. It is always through the Spirit that the blood possesses its living power in heaven and in the hearts of men.

The Power of the Blood of Christ

The blood and the Spirit always bear testimony together. Where the blood is honored in faith or preaching, there the Spirit works; and where He works, He always leads souls to the blood. The Holy Spirit could not be given until the blood was shed. The living bond between the Spirit and the blood cannot be broken.

It should be seriously noticed that, if the full power of the blood is to be manifested in our souls, we must place ourselves under the teaching of the Holy Spirit.

We must firmly believe that He is in us, carrying on His work in our hearts. We must live as those who know that the Spirit of God really dwells within, as a seed of life, and that He will bring the hidden, powerful effects of the blood to perfection. We must allow Him to lead us.

Through the Spirit, the blood will cleanse us, sanctify us, and unite us to God. When Peter wanted to urge believers to listen to God's voice with His call to holiness, *"Be ye holy; for I am holy"* (1 Peter 1:16), he reminded them that they had been redeemed by the precious blood of Christ.

Knowledge

His readers had to know that they had been redeemed and what that redemption signified; but above all, they had to know that it was not *"with corruptible things, as silver and gold"* (verse 18), things in which there was no power of life, *"but with the precious blood of Christ"* (verse 19). To have a correct perception of what the preciousness of that blood was (as the power of a perfect redemption) would be to them the power of a new and holy life.

Beloved Christians, this statement also applies to us. We must know that we are redeemed by *"the precious blood."* We must know about redemption and the blood before we can experience its power.

As we more fully understand what redemption is, and what the power and preciousness of the blood are by which redemption has been obtained, we will more fully experience its value.

Need and Desire

Let us take ourselves to the school of the Holy Spirit to be led into a deeper knowledge of redemption through the precious blood. Two things are needed for this: first, a deeper sense of need; and second, a desire to understand the blood better. The blood has been shed to take away sin. The power of the blood is to nullify the power of sin.

The blood cleanses, sanctifies, and unites us to God.

We are, unfortunately, too easily satisfied with the first beginnings of deliverance from sin. Oh, that what remains of sin in us might become unbearable to us! May we no longer be contented with the fact that we, as redeemed ones, sin against God's will in so many things.

May the desire for holiness become stronger in us. Should not the thought that the blood has more power than we know of, and can do for us greater things than we have yet experienced, cause our hearts to go out in strong desire? If there were more desire for deliverance from sin, for holiness and intimate friendship with a holy God, it would be the first thing that is necessary for being led further into knowledge of what the blood can do.

The Power of the Blood of Christ

Expectation

The second thing will follow. Desire must become expectation.

As we inquire from the Word, in faith, what the blood has accomplished, it must be a settled matter with us that the blood can manifest its full power also in us. No sense of unworthiness, ignorance, or helplessness must cause us to doubt. The blood works in the surrendered soul with a ceaseless power of life.

Surrender yourself to God the Holy Spirit.

Fix the eyes of your heart on the blood.

Open your whole inner being to its power.

Take shelter under the ever continuing sprinkling of the blood. The blood on which the throne of grace in heaven is founded can make your heart the temple and throne of God.

Ask the Lamb of God Himself to make the blood effective in you.

You will surely experience that there is nothing to compare with the wonder-working power of the blood of Jesus.

three
Reconciliation through the Blood

three

Reconciliation through the Blood

*Being justified freely by his grace through the redemption
that is in Christ Jesus: whom God hath set forth to be a
propitiation* [reconciliation] *through faith in his blood.*
—Romans 3:24–25

As we have seen, several distinct blessings have been procured for us by the power of the blood of Jesus, which are all included in the one word *"redemption."* Among these blessings, reconciliation takes the first place. *"God hath set forth* [Jesus] *to be a* [reconciliation] *through faith in his blood."* In our Lord's work of redemption, reconciliation naturally comes first. It stands first also among the things that must be done by the sinner who desires to have a share in redemption. Through it, a participation in the other blessings of redemption is made possible.

Also of great importance is that the believer, who has already received reconciliation, should obtain a deeper and more spiritual idea of its meaning and blessedness. If the power of the blood in redemption is rooted in reconciliation, then a fuller knowledge of reconciliation is the surest way to obtain a fuller experience of the power of the blood.

Reconciliation through the Blood

The heart that is surrendered to the teaching of the Holy Spirit will surely learn what reconciliation means. May our hearts be opened wide to receive it.

To understand what reconciliation by the blood means, let us consider the following:

- First, it is sin that has made reconciliation necessary
- Second, it is God's holiness that foreordained reconciliation
- Third, it is the blood of Jesus that obtained it
- Last, there is pardon that results from it

Sin Made Reconciliation Necessary

In all the work of Christ—and above all, in reconciliation—God's objective is the removal and destruction of sin. Knowledge of sin is necessary for the knowledge of reconciliation.

We need to understand what there is in sin that needs reconciliation and how reconciliation renders sin powerless. Then faith has something to take hold of, and the experience of that blessing is made possible.

Sin has had a twofold effect. It has had an effect on God, as well as on man. We generally emphasize its effect on man. But the effect it has exercised on God is more terrible and serious. Because of this effect on God, sin has its power over us. God, as Lord of all, could not overlook sin. It is His unalterable law that sin must bring forth sorrow and death. When man fell into sin, he, by that law of God, was brought under the power of sin. Thus, redemption must begin with the law of God, for if sin is made powerless against God, and the law of God gives sin no authority over us, then its power over us is destroyed. The knowledge that sin is speechless before God assures us that it no longer has authority over us.

What, then, was the effect of sin upon God? In His divine nature, He ever remains unchanged and unchangeable, but in His relationship and conduct toward man, an entire change has taken place. Sin is disobedience, a contempt of the authority of God; it seeks to rob God of His honor as God and Lord. Sin is determined opposition to a holy God. It not only can, but it must, awaken His wrath.

In the work of Christ, God's objective is the removal and destruction of sin.

While it was God's desire to continue in love and friendship with man, sin has compelled Him to become an opponent. Although the love of God toward man remains unchanged, sin made it impossible for Him to allow man to have fellowship with Himself. It has compelled Him to pour out upon man His wrath and curse and punishment, instead of His love. The change that sin has caused in God's relationship to man is enormous.

Man is guilty before God. Guilt is debt. We know what debt is. It is something that one person can demand from another, a claim that must be met and settled.

When sin is committed, its aftereffects may not be noticed, but its guilt remains. The sinner is guilty. God cannot disregard His own demand that sin must be punished; and His glory, which has been dishonored, must be upheld. As long as the debt is not discharged, or the guilt expiated, it is, in the nature of the case, impossible for a holy God to allow the sinner to come into His presence.

We often think that the great question for us is how we can be delivered from the indwelling power of sin, but that is a question of less importance than how we can be delivered from the guilt that is heaped up before God. Can the guilt of sin be removed? Can the effect of sin upon God, in awakening His wrath, be removed? Can sin be blotted out before God? If these things can be done, the power of sin will be broken in us also. The guilt of sin can be removed only through reconciliation.

The word translated as "reconciliation" means actually "to cover." Even heathen people had an idea of this. But in Israel, God revealed a reconciliation that could so truly cover and remove the guilt of sin that the original relationship between God and man can be entirely restored. This is what true reconciliation must do. It must so remove the guilt of sin, which is the effect of sin on God, that man can draw near to God in the blessed assurance that there is no longer the least guilt resting on him to keep him away from God.

Reconciliation Foreordained by the Holiness of God

If we are to understand reconciliation correctly, we must also consider the holiness of God that foreordained it. God's holiness is His infinite, glorious perfection, which leads Him always to desire what is good in others as well as in Himself. He bestows and works out what is good in others, and He hates and condemns all that is opposed to what is good.

In His holiness, both the love and wrath of God are united: His love bestows itself, and according to the divine law of righteousness, His wrath casts out and consumes what is evil. It is as the Holy One that God ordained reconciliation in Israel and took up His abode on the mercy seat. It is as the Holy One that He, in expectation of New Testament times, so often called Himself *"thy redeemer, the Holy One of Israel."* (See, for example, Isaiah 41:14.) It is as the Holy One that God worked out His plan of reconciliation in Christ.

Can the guilt of sin be removed? Yes!

The wonder of this plan is that both the holy love and the holy wrath of God find satisfaction in it. Apparently they were in irreconcilable strife with one another. The holy love was unwilling to let man go. Notwithstanding all his sin, it could not give him up. He had to be redeemed. The holy wrath, likewise, could not surrender its demands. The law had been despised; God had been dishonored. God's rights had to be upheld. There could be no thought of releasing the sinner as long as the law was not satisfied. The terrible effect of sin on God had to be counteracted; the guilt of sin had to be removed; otherwise the sinner could not be delivered. The only possible solution was reconciliation.

We have seen that reconciliation means covering. It means that something else has taken the place where sin was established so that sin can no longer be seen by God.

But because God is the Holy One and *"His eyes* [are] *as a flame of fire"* (Revelation 1:14), that which covered sin must be something of such a nature that it really counteracted the evil that sin had done, and also that it blotted out sin before God so that it was really destroyed and was not now to be seen.

Reconciliation for sin can take place only by satisfaction. Satisfaction is reconciliation. And as satisfaction is through a substitute, sin can be punished and the sinner can be saved. God's holiness also would be glorified and its demands would be met. The demand of God's love would be satisfied in the redemption of the sinner, and the demand of His righteousness would be satisfied in the maintenance of the glory of God and of His law.

We know how this was set forth in the Old Testament laws of the offerings. A clean animal took the place of a guilty man. His sin was laid, by confession, on the head of the animal, which bore the punishment by surrendering its life unto death. Then the blood, representing a clean life that now, through the bearing of punishment, is free from guilt, can be brought into God's presence; the blood, or life, of the animal has borne the punishment in place of the sinner. That blood made reconciliation and covered the sinner and his sin because it had taken his place and atoned for his sin.

There was reconciliation in the blood. But that was not a reality. The blood of cattle or of goats could never take away sin; it was only a shadow, a picture, of the real reconciliation.

Blood of a totally different character was necessary for an effective covering of guilt. According to the plan of the holy God, nothing less than the blood of God's own Son could bring about reconciliation. Righteousness demanded it; love offered it. *"Being justified freely by his grace through the redemption that is in Christ Jesus: whom God hath set forth to be a propitiation* [reconciliation] *through faith in his blood."*

Reconciliation Obtained by the Blood of Jesus

Our third point of consideration is that reconciliation must satisfy the demands of God's holy law. The Lord Jesus accomplished this. By a willing and perfect obedience, He fulfilled the law under which He had placed Himself. In the same spirit of complete surrender to the will of the Father, He bore the curse that the law had pronounced against sin. He rendered, in fullest measure of obedience or punishment, all that the law of God could ever ask or desire. The law was perfectly satisfied by Him. But how can His fulfilling of the demands of the law be reconciliation for the sins of others? Because, both in creation and in the holy covenant of grace that the Father had made with Him, He was recognized as the Head of the human race.

Satisfaction is reconciliation.

Because of this, He was able, by becoming flesh, to become the Second Adam. When He, the Word, became flesh, He placed Himself in a real fellowship with our flesh, which was under the power of sin, and He assumed the responsibility for everything that sin had done in the flesh against God. His perfection and obedience were not merely those of one man among others, but those of Him who had placed Himself in fellowship with all other men and who had taken their sin upon Himself.

As Head of mankind through creation, as their representative in the covenant, He became their surety. As a perfect satisfaction of the demands of the law was accomplished by the shedding of His blood, this was the reconciliation, the covering, of our sin.

Above all, we must never forget that He was God. This bestowed a divine power on Him to unite Himself with His creatures and to take them up into Himself. It bestowed on His sufferings a virtue of infinite holiness and power. It made the merit of His bloodshedding more than sufficient to deal with all the guilt of human sin. It made His blood such a real reconciliation, such a perfect covering of sin, that the holiness of God no longer beholds it. Sin has been, in truth, blotted out. The blood of Jesus, God's Son, has procured a real, perfect, and eternal reconciliation.

What does this mean?

I have spoken of the awful effect of sin on God, of the terrible change that took place in heaven through sin. Instead of favor, friendship, blessing, and the life of God from heaven, man had nothing to look for except wrath, curse, death, and perdition. He could think of God only with fear and terror, without hope, and without love. Sin never ceased to call for vengeance; guilt had to be dealt with in full.

But see! The blood of Jesus, God's Son, has been shed. Atonement for sin has been made. Peace is restored. A change has taken place again, as real and widespread as that which sin had brought about. For those who receive the reconciliation, sin has been brought to nothing. The wrath of God turns around and hides itself in the depth of divine love.

The righteousness of God no longer terrifies man. It meets him as a friend, with an offer of complete justification. God's countenance beams with pleasure and approval as the penitent sinner draws near to Him, and He invites him to intimate fellowship. He opens for him a treasure of blessing. There is nothing now that can separate him from God (Romans 8:38–39).

Sin has been blotted out by the blood of Jesus.

The reconciliation through the blood of Jesus has covered his sins; they no longer appear in God's sight. God no longer attributes sin to him. Reconciliation has brought out a perfect and eternal redemption.

Oh, who can tell the worth of this precious blood?

It is no wonder that mention will forever be made of that blood in the song of the redeemed, and through all eternity. As long as heaven lasts, the praise of the blood will resound: *"Thou wast slain, and hast redeemed us to God by thy blood"* (Revelation 5:9).

But here is the wonder: that the redeemed on earth do not more heartily join in that song and that they are not abounding in praise for the reconciliation that the power of the blood has accomplished.

Pardon Follows Reconciliation

That the blood has made reconciliation for sin and covered it, and that as a result of this, such a wonderful change has taken place in the heavenly realms—all this will avail us nothing unless we obtain a personal share in it.

It is in the pardon of sin that this takes place. God has offered a perfect acquittal from all our sin and guilt.

Reconciliation through the Blood

Because reconciliation has been made for sin, we can now be reconciled to Him. *"God was in Christ, reconciling the world unto himself, not imputing their trespasses unto them"* (2 Corinthians 5:19). Following this word of reconciliation is the invitation, *"Be ye reconciled to God"* (verse 20). Whoever receives reconciliation for sin is reconciled to God. He knows that all his sins are forgiven.

The Scriptures use many illustrations to emphasize the fullness of forgiveness and to convince the fearful heart of the sinner that the blood has really taken his sin away. *"I have blotted out, as a thick cloud, thy transgressions, and, as a cloud, thy sins"* (Isaiah 44:22). *"Thou hast cast all my sins behind thy back"* (Isaiah 38:17). *"Thou wilt cast all their sins into the depths of the sea"* (Micah 7:19). *"The iniquity of Israel shall be sought for, and there shall be none; and the sins of Judah, and they shall not be found: for I will pardon them whom I reserve"* (Jeremiah 50:20).

This is what the New Testament calls *justification.* It is thus named in Romans 3:23–26:

For all have sinned...being justified freely [for nothing] *by His grace through the redemption that is in Christ Jesus: whom God hath set forth to be a propitiation through faith in his blood, to declare his righteousness...that he might be just, and the justifier of him which believeth in Jesus.*

So perfect is the reconciliation, and so really has sin been covered and blotted out, that he who believes in Christ is looked upon, and treated by God, as entirely righteous. The acquittal that he has received from God is so complete that there is nothing, absolutely nothing, to prevent him from approaching God with the utmost freedom.

The Power of the Blood of Christ

For the enjoyment of this blessedness, nothing is necessary except faith in the blood. The blood alone has done everything.

The penitent sinner who turns from his sin to God needs only faith in that blood. That is, he needs only faith in the power of the blood, that it has truly atoned for sin and that it really has atoned for him. Through that faith, he knows that he is fully reconciled to God and that there is now not the least thing to hinder God's pouring out on him the fullness of His love and blessing.

Whoever receives reconciliation is completely forgiven.

If he looks toward heaven, which formerly was covered with clouds, black with God's wrath, and a coming awful judgment, those clouds are no longer to be seen; everything is bright in the glad light of God's face and God's love. Faith in the blood manifests in his heart the same wonder-working power that it exercised in heaven. Through faith in the blood, he becomes partaker of all the blessings that the blood has obtained for him from God.

Fellow believers, pray earnestly that the Holy Spirit may reveal to you the glory of this reconciliation and the pardon of your sins, made yours through the blood of Jesus. Pray for enlightened hearts to see how completely the accusing and condemning power of your sin has been removed and how God, in the fullness of His love and good pleasure, has turned toward you. Open your hearts to the Holy Spirit so that He may reveal in you the glorious effects that the blood has had in heaven. God has set forth Jesus Christ Himself as a reconciliation through faith in His blood. He is the reconciliation for our sins. Rely on Him as having already covered your sin before God. Set Him between yourself and your sins, and you will experience how complete the redemption is that He has accomplished, and how powerful the reconciliation is through faith in His blood.

Then, through the living Christ, the powerful effects that the blood has brought about in heaven will increasingly be manifested in your hearts, and you will know what it means to walk, by the Spirit's grace, in the full light and enjoyment of forgiveness.

And you who have not yet obtained forgiveness of your sins, does this word not come to you as an urgent call to faith in His blood? Will you never allow yourself to be moved by what God has done for you as a sinner? *"Herein is love, not that we loved God, but that he loved us, and sent his Son to be the propitiation for our sins"* (1 John 4:10).

The precious blood divine has been shed; reconciliation is complete; and the message comes to you, *"Be reconciled to God"* (2 Corinthians 5:20).

If you repent of your sins, and if you desire to be delivered from sin's power and bondage, exercise faith in the blood. Open your heart to the influence of the word that God has sent to be spoken to you. Open your heart to the message, so that the blood can deliver you—yes, even you—this moment. Only believe it. Say, "This blood is also for me." If you come as a guilty, lost sinner, longing for pardon, you may rest assured that the blood, which has already made a perfect reconciliation, immediately covers your sin and restores you to the favor and love of God.

The Power of the Blood of Christ

So I urge you, exercise faith in the blood. This moment bow down before God and tell Him that you do believe in the power of the blood for your own soul. Having said that, stand by it; cling to it. Through faith in His blood, Jesus Christ will be the reconciliation for your sins also.

four
Cleansing through the Blood

four

Cleansing through the Blood

If we walk in the light, as he is in the light, we have fellowship one with another, and the blood of Jesus Christ his Son cleanseth us from all sin.
—1 John 1:7

We have seen that the most important effect of the blood is reconciliation for sin. But this first effect of the blood is not the only one. The more the soul, through faith, yields itself to the Spirit of God to understand and enjoy the full power of reconciliation, the more power the blood exerts in imparting the other blessings that, in Scripture, are attributed to it.

One of the first results of reconciliation is cleansing from sin. Let us see what God's Word has to say about this. Cleansing is often spoken about among us as if it were no more than the pardon of sins, or the cleansing from guilt. This, however, is not so. Scripture does not speak of being cleansed from guilt. Cleansing from sin means deliverance from the pollution, not from the guilt, of sin. The guilt of sin concerns our relationship to God and our responsibility to make good for our misdoings (or to bear the punishment of them). The pollution of sin, on the other hand, is the sense of defilement and impurity that sin brings to our inner beings, and cleansing has to do with this.

It is of the greatest importance, for every believer who desires to enjoy the full salvation that God has provided for him, to understand correctly what the Scriptures teach about this cleansing. Let us consider the following:

- First, what does the word *cleansing* mean in the Old Testament?

- Second, what is the blessing indicated by this word in the New Testament?

- Third, how may we experience the full enjoyment of this blessing?

Cleansing in the Old Testament

In the service of God as ordained by the hand of Moses for Israel, there were two ceremonies to be observed by God's people in preparation for approaching to Him. These were the offerings, or sacrifices, and the cleansings, or purifications. Both were to be observed but in different manners. Both were intended to remind man how sinful he was and how unfit to draw near to a holy God. Both were to typify the redemption by which the Lord Jesus Christ would restore fellowship with God to man. As a rule, only the offerings are regarded as typical of redemption through Christ. The epistle to the Hebrews, however, emphatically mentions the cleansings as symbols *"for the time then present, in which were offered... sacrifices...and divers washings"* (Hebrews 9:9–10).

The Power of the Blood of Christ

If we can imagine the life of an Israelite, we will understand that the consciousness of sin and the need for redemption were awakened no less by the cleansings than the offerings. We must also learn from them what the power of the blood of Jesus actually is.

Through reconciliation, we are cleansed from sin.

We may take one of the more important cases of cleansing as an illustration. If anyone was in a hut or house where a dead body lay, or if he had even touched a dead body or bones, he was unclean for seven days. Death, as the punishment for sin, made everyone who came into association with it unclean. Cleansing was accomplished by using the ashes of a young heifer that had been burned, as described in Numbers 19. (Compare Hebrews 9:13–14.) These ashes, mixed with water, were sprinkled by means of a bunch of hyssop on the one who was unclean; he then had to bathe himself in water, after which he was once more ceremonially clean.

The words *unclean, cleansing,* and *clean* were also used in reference to the healing of leprosy, a disease that might be described as a living death. Here, he who was to be cleansed had to bathe in water, having been first sprinkled with water, in which the blood of a bird, sacrificially offered, had been mixed. Seven days later, he was again sprinkled with sacrificial blood. (See Leviticus 13 and 14.)

An attentive contemplation of the laws of cleansing will teach us that the difference between the cleansings and the offerings was twofold. First, the offering had definite reference to the transgression for which reconciliation had to be made. Cleansing had more to do with conditions that were not sinful in themselves but were the result of sin and, therefore, had to be acknowledged by God's holy people as defiled. Second, in the case of the offering, nothing was done to the offerer himself. He saw the blood sprinkled on the altar or carried into the Holy Place; he had to believe that this procured reconciliation before God. But nothing was done to himself. In cleansing, on the other hand, what happened to the person was the chief thing. Defilement was something that, either through internal disease or outward touch, had come upon the man; so the washing or sprinkling with water had to take place on himself as ordained by God.

Cleansing was something that he could feel and experience. It brought about a change not only in his relationship to God but also in his own condition. In the offering, something was done for him; by cleansing, something was done in him. The offering had respect to his guilt; the cleansing, to the pollution of sin.

The same meaning of the words *clean* and *cleansing* is found elsewhere in the Old Testament. David prayed in Psalm 51, *"**Cleanse** me from my sin....Purge me with hyssop, and I shall be **clean**"* (verses 2, 7, emphasis added). The word used by David here is that which is used most frequently for the cleansing of anyone who had touched a dead body. Hyssop was also used in such cases. David prayed for more than pardon. He confessed that he had been *"shapen in iniquity"* (verse 5), that his nature was sinful. He prayed that he might be made pure within. *"**Cleanse** me from my sin"* was his prayer. He used the same word later on in the same psalm when he prayed, *"Create in me a **clean** heart, O God"* (verse 10, emphasis added). Cleansing is more than pardon.

Cleansing is something to be felt and experienced.

In the same manner, this word was used by Ezekiel and refers to an inner condition that must be changed. This is evident from Ezekiel 24:13, where, speaking of uncleanness being melted out, God said, *"Because I have purged thee, and thou wast not purged."* Later on, in Ezekiel 36:25, speaking of the new covenant, He said, *"Then will I sprinkle clean water upon you, and ye shall be clean: from all your filthiness, and from all your idols."*

Malachi used the same word, connecting it with fire: *"He shall sit as a refiner and purifier of silver: and he shall purify* [cleanse] *the sons of Levi"* (Malachi 3:3).

Cleansing by water, by blood, and by fire are all typical of the cleansing that would take place under the new covenant—an inner cleansing and deliverance from the stain of sin.

Cleansing as Blessing in the New Testament

Mention is often made in the New Testament of a clean or pure heart. Our Lord said, *"Blessed are the pure in heart"* (Matthew 5:8).

Paul spoke of *"charity out of a pure heart"* (1 Timothy 1:5). He also spoke of *"a pure conscience"* (1 Timothy 3:9).

Cleansing through the Blood

Peter exhorted his readers to *"love one another with a pure heart fervently"* (1 Peter 1:22). The word *cleansing* is also implied in this same verse: *"Ye have purified your souls."*

We read of those who are described as "God's people," that God purified, or cleansed, their hearts through faith (Acts 15:9).

The purpose of the Lord Jesus concerning those who were His was to *"purify* [cleanse] *unto himself a peculiar people"* (Titus 2:14).

Regarding ourselves, we read, *"Let us cleanse ourselves from all filthiness of the flesh and spirit"* (2 Corinthians 7:1).

All these places teach us that cleansing is an inward work in the heart and that it is subsequent to pardon.

We are told in 1 John 1:7 that *"the blood of Jesus Christ his Son cleanseth us from all sin."* This word, *"cleanseth,"* does not refer to the grace of pardon received at conversion but to the effect of grace in God's children who walk in the light. We read, *"If we walk in the light, as he is in the light, we have fellowship one with another, and the blood of Jesus Christ his Son cleanseth us from all sin."* That it refers to something more than pardon appears from what follows in verse 9: *"He is faithful and just to forgive us our sins, and to cleanse us from all unrighteousness."* Cleansing is something that comes after pardon and is the result of it, by the inward and experiential reception of the power of the blood of Jesus in the heart of the believer.

This takes place according to the Word, first in the purifying of the conscience. *"How much more shall the blood of Christ...purge your conscience from dead works to serve the living God?"* (Hebrews 9:14). The mention already made of the ashes of a heifer sprinkling the unclean typifies a personal experience of the precious blood of Christ. Conscience is not only a judge to give sentence on our actions; it is also the inward voice that bears witness to our relationship to God, and to God's relationship to us. When it is cleansed by the blood, then it bears witness that we are well-pleasing to God.

When the conscience is cleansed, so is the heart.

It is written in Hebrews 10:2, *"The worshipers once purged should have had no more conscience of sins."* Through the Spirit, we receive an inward experience that the blood has so fully delivered us from the guilt and power of sin that we, in our regenerated nature, have escaped entirely from its dominion (Romans 6:14). Sin still dwells in our flesh, with its temptations, but it has no power to rule. The conscience is cleansed; there is no need for the least shadow of separation between God and us; we look up to Him in the full power of redemption. The conscience cleansed by the blood bears witness to nothing less than a complete redemption, the fullness of God's good pleasure.

And if the conscience is cleansed, so also is the heart, of which the conscience is the center. We read of having a heart cleansed from an evil conscience (Hebrews 10:22). Not only must the conscience be cleansed, but the heart also must be cleansed, including the understanding and the will, with all our thoughts and desires. Through the blood, by the shedding of which Christ delivered Himself up to death and by virtue of which He entered again into heaven, the death and resurrection of Christ are ceaselessly effective. By this power of His death and resurrection, sinful lusts and inclinations are slain.

"The blood of Jesus Christ his Son cleanseth us from all sin" (1 John 1:7)—from original, as well as actual, sin. The blood exercises its spiritual, heavenly power in the soul. The believer in whose life the blood is fully effective knows that his old nature is hindered from manifesting its power. Through the blood, its lusts and desires are subdued and slain, and everything is cleansed so that the Spirit can bring forth His glorious fruit. In case of the least stumbling, the soul finds immediate cleansing and restoration. Even unconscious sins are rendered powerless.

We have noted a difference between the guilt and the pollution of sin. This is of importance for a clear understanding of the matter, but in actual life, we must ever remember that they are not thus divided. Through the blood, God deals with sin as a whole. Every true operation of the blood manifests its power simultaneously over the guilt and the pollution of sin. Reconciliation and cleansing always go together, and the blood is ceaselessly operative.

Many seem to think that the blood is there so that, if we have sinned again, we can turn again to it to be cleansed. But this is not so. Just as a fountain flows always, and always purifies what is placed in it or under its stream, so it is with this fountain, opened *"for sin and for uncleanness"* (Zechariah 13:1). The eternal power of life of the eternal Spirit works through the blood. Through Him, the heart can abide always under the flow and cleansing of the blood.

In the Old Testament, cleansing was necessary for each sin. In the New Testament, cleansing depends on Him who ever lives to intercede (Hebrews 7:25). When faith sees and desires and lays hold of this fact, the heart can abide every moment under the protecting and cleansing power of the blood.

Experiencing the Full Enjoyment of This Blessing

Everyone who, through faith, obtains a share in the atoning merit of the blood of Christ also has a share in its cleansing power. But the experience of its power to cleanse is, for several reasons, sadly imperfect. It is therefore of great importance to understand what the conditions are for the full enjoyment of this glorious blessing.

First of all, knowledge is necessary. Many think that pardon of sin is all that we receive through the blood. They ask for and so obtain nothing more.

It is a blessed thing to begin to see that the Holy Spirit of God has a special purpose in making use of different words in Scripture concerning the effects of the blood. Then we begin to inquire about their special meaning. Let everyone who truly longs to know what the Lord desires to teach us by this one word, *cleansing*, attentively compare all the places in Scripture where the word is used, where cleansing is spoken of. He will soon feel that there is more promised to the believer than the removal of guilt. He will begin to understand that cleansing through washing can take away stain, and although he cannot fully explain in what way this takes place, he will, however, be convinced that he may expect a blessed inward operation of the cleansing away of the effects of sin by the blood. Knowledge of this fact is the first condition of experiencing it.

Second, there must be desire. It is to be feared that our Christianity is only too pleased to postpone to a future life the experience of the beatitude that our Lord intended for our earthly lives: *"Blessed are the pure in heart: for they shall see God"* (Matthew 5:8).

The heart can abide every moment under the protecting and cleansing power of the blood.

It is not sufficiently recognized that purity of heart is a characteristic of every child of God, that it is the necessary condition of fellowship with Him, of the enjoyment of His salvation. There is too little inner longing to be truly in all things, at all times, well-pleasing to the Lord. Sin and the stain of sin trouble us too little.

God's Word comes to us with the promise of blessing that ought to awaken all our desires. Believe that the blood of Jesus cleanses from all sin. If you learn how to yield yourself correctly to its operation, it can do great things in you. Should you not desire every hour to experience its glorious cleansing effectiveness; to be preserved, in spite of your depraved nature, from the many stains for which your conscience is constantly accusing you? May your desires be awakened to long for this blessing. Put God to the test to work out in you what He, as the Faithful One, has promised—cleansing *"from all unrighteousness"* (1 John 1:9).

The Power of the Blood of Christ

The third condition is a willingness to separate yourself from everything that is unclean. Through sin, everything in our natures and in the world is defiled. Cleansing cannot take place where there is not an entire separation from, and giving up of, everything unclean. *"Touch not the unclean thing"* (2 Corinthians 6:17) is God's command to His chosen ones. I must recognize that all the things surrounding me are unclean.

My friends, my possessions, my spirit must all be surrendered so that I may be cleansed in each relationship by the precious blood and so that all the activities of my spirit, soul, and being may experience a thorough cleansing.

He who will keep back anything, however small, cannot obtain the full blessing. He who is willing to pay the full price, so as to have his whole being baptized by the blood, is on the way to understand fully this word: *"The blood of Jesus...cleanseth us from all sin"* (1 John 1:7).

The last condition is exercising faith in the power of the blood. It is not as if we, through our faith, give the blood its effectiveness. No, the blood always retains its power and effectiveness, but our unbelief closes our hearts and hinders its operation. Faith is simply the removal of that hindrance, the setting open of our hearts, for the divine power by which the living Lord will bestow His blood.

Yes, let us believe that there is cleansing through the blood.

You have perhaps seen a spring in the midst of a patch of grass. From the much traveled road that runs by that patch, dust is constantly falling over the grass that grows by the side of the road. But where the water from the spring falls in a refreshing and cleansing spray, there is no sign of dust, and everything is green and fresh. Similarly, the precious blood of Christ carries on its blessed work without ceasing in the soul of the believer who, by faith, takes hold of it. For him who, by faith, commits himself to the Lord and believes that this can and will take place, it will be given to him.

The blood always retains its power and effectiveness.

The heavenly, spiritual effect of the blood can be really experienced every moment. Its power is such that I can always abide in the fountain, always dwell in the wounds of my Lord.

Believer, come, I entreat you; put to the test how the blood of Jesus can cleanse your heart from all sin.

You know with what joy a weary traveler would bathe in a fresh stream, plunging into the water to experience its cooling, cleansing, strengthening effect. Lift up your eyes and see by faith how ceaselessly a stream flows from heaven above to earth beneath. It is the blessed Spirit's influence, through whom the power of the blood of Jesus flows earthward over souls, to heal and to purify them. Oh, place yourself in this stream; simply believe that the words *"the blood of Jesus...cleanseth us from all sin"* (1 John 1:7) have a divine meaning—deeper, wider, than you have ever imagined. Believe that it is the Lord Jesus Himself who will cleanse you in His blood and fulfill His promise in power in you. And consider the cleansing from sin by His blood as a blessing, in the daily enjoyment of which you can confidently abide.

five
Sanctification through the Blood

Sanctification through the Blood

*Wherefore Jesus also, that he might sanctify the people with
his own blood, suffered without the gate.*
—Hebrews 13:12

To a superficial observer, it might seem that there is
little difference between cleansing and sanctification, that the two words mean about the same thing.
But the difference is great and important. As I indicated in
the previous chapter, cleansing has to do chiefly with the
old life and the stain of sin that must be removed. It is only
a preparatory work. Sanctification, on the other hand, concerns the new life and the characteristic of it that must be
imparted to it by God. Sanctification, which means "union
with God," is the fullness of blessing purchased for us by
the blood.

The distinction between these two things is clearly
marked in Scripture. Paul reminded us that *"Christ also
loved the church, and gave himself for it; that he might
sanctify and cleanse it"* (Ephesians 5:25–26). Having first
cleansed it, He then sanctifies it. Writing to Timothy, Paul
said, *"If a man therefore purge himself...he shall be a*

Sanctification through the Blood

vessel unto honour, sanctified, and meet for the master's use." (2 Timothy 2:21). Sanctification is a blessing that follows, and surpasses, cleansing.

Sanctification is also strikingly illustrated by the ordinances connected to the consecration of the priests compared with that of the Levites. In the case of the Levites, who took a lower position than the priests in the service of the sanctuary, no mention is made of sanctification, but the term *cleanse* is used four times in relation to them in Numbers 8. In the consecration of the priests, on the other hand, the word *sanctify is* often used, for the priests stood in a closer relationship to God than the Levites. (See Exodus 29; Leviticus 8.)

At the same time, this record emphasizes the close connection between sanctification and the sacrificial blood. In the case of the consecration of the Levites, reconciliation for sin was made and they were sprinkled with the water of purification for cleansing—but they were not sprinkled with blood. In the consecration of the priests, however, blood had to be sprinkled upon them. They were sanctified by a more personal and intimate application of the blood.

All this was a foreshadowing of the sanctification through the blood of Jesus, and this is what we now seek to understand, so that we may obtain a share in it. Let us then consider:

- First, what sanctification is
- Second, that it was the great purpose of the sufferings of Christ
- Last, that sanctification can be obtained through the blood

What Sanctification Is

To understand what the sanctification of the redeemed is, we must first learn what the holiness of God is. He alone is the Holy One. Holiness in the creature must be received from Him as a gift.

God alone is the Holy One.

God's holiness is often spoken of as though it consisted in His hatred of, and hostility toward, sin; but this gives no explanation of what holiness actually is. It is merely a negative statement—that God's holiness cannot bear sin.

Holiness is the attribute of God that causes Him always to will and do what is supremely good. Because of His holiness, He desires what is supremely good in His creatures and bestows it upon them.

God is called *"the Holy One"* (2 Kings 19:22, for example) in Scripture not only because He punishes sin but also because He is the Redeemer of His people. It is His holiness, which ever wills what is good for all, that moved Him to redeem sinners. Both the wrath of God that punishes sin and love of God that redeems the sinner spring from the same source—His holiness. Holiness is the perfection of God's nature.

Holiness in man is a disposition in entire agreement with that of God, which chooses in all things to will as God wills, as it is written: *"As he which hath called you is holy, so be ye holy in all manner of conversation"* (1 Peter 1:15). Holiness in us is nothing else than oneness with God. The sanctification of God's people is brought about by the communication to them of the holiness of God. There is no way of obtaining sanctification except by the holy God bestowing what He alone possesses. He alone is the Holy One. He is the Lord who sanctifies.

By the different meanings that Scripture attaches to the words *sanctification* and *to sanctify,* a certain relationship with God, into which we are brought, is pointed out.

The simplest meaning of *sanctification* is separation.

The first and simplest meaning of the word *sanctification* is separation. That which is taken out of its surroundings, by God's command, and is set aside or separated as His own possession and for His service—that thing is holy. This does not mean separation from sin only but from all that is in the world, even from what may be permissible. (See 1 Corinthians 6:12.) Thus God sanctified the seventh day. The other days were not unclean, for God saw all that He had made and *"behold, it was very good"* (Genesis 1:31). But that day alone was holy because God had taken possession of it by His own special act. In the same way, God had separated Israel from other nations and, in Israel, had separated the priests, to be holy unto Him. This separation unto sanctification is always God's own work, and so the electing grace of God is often closely connected with sanctification. *"And ye shall be holy unto me: for I...have severed you from other people, that ye should be mine"* (Leviticus 20:26). *"The man whom the LORD doth choose, he shall be holy"* (Numbers 16:7). *"thou art an holy people unto the LORD thy God: the LORD thy God hath chosen thee"* (Deuteronomy 7:6). God cannot take part with other lords.

He must be the sole possessor and ruler of those to whom He reveals and imparts His holiness.

But this separation is not all that is included in the word *sanctification*. It is only the indispensable condition of what must follow. When separated, man stands before God in no respect differing from an inanimate object that has been sanctified to the service of God. If the separation is to be of value, something more must take place. Man must surrender himself willingly and heartily to this separation. Sanctification includes personal consecration to the Lord to be His.

Sanctification can become ours only when it sends down its roots into and takes up its abode in the depths of our personal lives, our wills, and our love. God sanctifies no man against his will; therefore, the personal, hearty surrender to God is an indispensable part of sanctification.

It is for this reason that the Scriptures not only speak of God sanctifying us, but they say often that we must sanctify ourselves.

But even by consecration, true sanctification is not yet complete. Separation and consecration are together only the preparation for the glorious work that God will do as He imparts His own holiness to the soul. Partaking of the divine nature is the blessing that is promised to believers in sanctification. *"That we might be partakers of his holiness"* (Hebrews 12:10)—this is the glorious aim of God's work in those whom He separates for Himself. But this impartation of His holiness is not a gift of something that is apart from God Himself. No! It is in personal fellowship with Him and in partaking of His divine life that sanctification can be obtained.

Sanctification through the Blood

As the Holy One, God dwelt among the people of Israel to sanctify His people (Exodus 29:45–46). As the Holy One, He dwells in us. It is the presence of God alone that can sanctify. But so surely is this our portion that Scripture does not shrink from speaking of God's dwelling in our hearts in such power that we may be *"filled with all the fulness of God"* (Ephesians 3:19). True sanctification is fellowship with God and His dwelling in us. So it was necessary that God, in Christ, should take up His abode in the flesh, and that the Holy Spirit should come to dwell in us. This is what sanctification means.

Sanctification must send down roots and make its abode in the depths of our lives.

Sanctification as the Purpose for Which Christ Suffered

Christ suffered for the purpose of sanctification. This is plainly stated in Hebrews 13:12: *"Jesus also, that he might sanctify the people with his own blood, suffered."* In the wisdom of God, a participation in His holiness is the highest destiny of man. Therefore, this was the central purpose of our Lord Jesus' the coming to earth and, above all, of His sufferings and death. It was *"that He might sanctify the people"* (verse 12) and that they *"should be holy and without blame"* (Ephesians 1:4).

How the sufferings of Christ attained this end and became our sanctification is made plain to us by the words He spoke to His Father when He was about to allow Himself to be bound as a sacrifice. *"For their sakes I sanctify myself, that they also might be sanctified through the truth"*

(John 17:19). Because His sufferings and death were a sanctification of Himself, they can become sanctification for us.

What does this mean? Jesus was *"the Holy One of God"* (Mark 1:24; Luke 4:34). He was *"him, whom the Father hath sanctified, and sent into the world"* (John 10:36). Did He have to sanctify Himself? He had to do so; it was indispensable.

The sanctification that He possessed was not beyond the reach of temptation. In His temptation, He had to maintain it and show how perfectly His will was surrendered to the holiness of God. We have seen that true holiness in man is the perfect oneness of his will with that of God. Throughout our Lord's life, from the temptation in the wilderness onward, He had subjected His will to the will of His Father and had consecrated Himself as a sacrifice to God. But it was chiefly in Gethsemane that He did this. There was the hour and the power of darkness; the temptation to put away the terrible cup of wrath from His lips and to do His own will came with almost irresistible power, but He rejected the temptation. He offered up Himself and His will to the will and holiness of God. He sanctified Himself by a perfect oneness of will with that of God.

This sanctification of Himself has become the power by which we also may be sanctified through the truth. This is in perfect accord with what we learn from the epistle to the Hebrews where, in reference to the words used by Christ, we read, *"I come to do thy will, O God"* (Hebrews 10:9), and then it is added, *"By the which will we are sanctified through the offering of the body of Jesus Christ once for all"* (verse 10). Because the offering of His body was

His surrender of Himself to do the will of God, we become sanctified by that will. He sanctified Himself there for us so that we might be sanctified through the truth. The perfect obedience in which He surrendered Himself, so that God's holy will might be accomplished in Him, was not only the meritorious cause of our salvation but is, at the same time, the power by which sin was forever conquered; it is also by this obedience that the same disposition, and the same sanctification, may be created in our own hearts.

Jesus had to sanctify Himself; it was indispensable.

Elsewhere in the book of Hebrews, the true relationship of our Lord to His own people is even more clearly characterized as having sanctification for its chief end. After we read of how fitting it was that our Lord suffered as He did, we find, *"For both he that sanctifieth and they who are sanctified are all of one"* (Hebrews 2:11). The unity between the Lord Jesus and His people consists in the fact that they both receive their life from one Father, and both have a share in one and the same sanctification. Jesus is the Sanctifier; they become the sanctified. Sanctification is the bond that unites them. *"Wherefore Jesus also, that he might sanctify the people with his own blood, suffered."*

If we are truly willing to understand and experience what sanctification by the blood means, then it is of the utmost importance for us to first lay hold of these facts: that sanctification is the characteristic and purpose of the entire sufferings of our Lord; and that, regarding those sufferings, the blood was the fruit and means of blessing. His sanctification of Himself has the characteristic of those sufferings, and therein lay its value and power. Our sanctification is the purpose of those sufferings, and it is only in order to attain that purpose that they work out the perfect blessing. The more this becomes clear to us, the more we will press forward into the true meaning and blessing of His sufferings.

It was as the Holy One that God foreordained redemption. It was His will to glorify His holiness in victory over sin by the sanctification of mankind after His own image. It was with the same purpose that our Lord Jesus endured and accomplished His sufferings; we must be consecrated to God. And if the Holy Spirit, the holy God as Spirit, comes into us to reveal in us the redemption that is in Jesus, this also continues to be the main purpose with Him. As the Holy Spirit, He is the Spirit of holiness.

The Holy Spirit is the Spirit of holiness.

Reconciliation, pardon, and cleansing from sin all have an unspeakable value; they all, however, point onward to sanctification. It is God's will that each one who has been marked by the precious blood should know that it is a divine mark, characterizing his entire separation to God; that this blood calls him to an undivided consecration to a life wholly for God; and that this blood is the promise and the power of a participation in God's holiness, through which God Himself will make His abiding place in him and be his God.

Sanctification through the Blood

Oh, that we might understand and believe that *"Jesus also, that he might sanctify the people with his own blood, suffered."*

How to Obtain Sanctification by the Blood

How can this sanctification be obtained? An answer to this question, in general, is that everyone who is a partaker of the virtue of the blood is also a partaker of sanctification and is in God's sight a sanctified person.

To the extent that he lives in close and abiding contact with the blood, he continues increasingly to experience its sanctifying effects, even though he still understands little of how those effects are produced. Let no one think that he must first understand how to take hold of or explain everything before he may, by faith, pray that the blood might manifest its sanctifying power in him. No, it was in connection with cleansing—the washing of the disciples' feet—that the Lord Jesus said, *"What I do thou knowest not now; but thou shalt know hereafter"* (John 13:7). It is the Lord Jesus Himself who sanctifies His people *"with His own blood."* He who heartily gives himself up to believing worship of and intimacy with the Lamb, who has bought us with His blood, will experience a sanctification beyond what he can imagine through that blood. The Lord Jesus will do this for him.

But the believer ought to grow in knowledge also; only in this way can he enter into the full blessing that is prepared for him. We not only have the right but also the duty to inquire earnestly what the essential connection is between the blessed effect of the blood and our sanctification, and in what way the Lord Jesus will work out in us, by His blood, those things that we have ascertained to be the chief qualities of sanctification.

We have seen that the beginning of all sanctification is separation to God as His entire possession, to be at His disposal. This is just what the blood proclaims: that the power of sin is broken; that we are loosed from its bonds; that we are no longer its bondservants but belong to Him who purchased our freedom with His blood. *"Ye are not your own....ye are bought with a price"* (1 Corinthians 6:19–20). This is the language in which the blood tells us that we are God's possession. Because He desires to have us entirely for Himself, He has chosen us, bought us, and set upon us the distinguishing mark of the blood, as those who are separated from everything around them to live only for His service.

The believer ought to grow in knowledge.

This idea of separation is clearly expressed in the words we so often repeat, *"Jesus also, that he might sanctify the people with his own blood, suffered without the gate. Let us go forth therefore unto him without the camp, bearing his reproach"* (Hebrews 13:12–13). Going forth from all that is of this world was the characteristic of Him who was holy, undefiled, separate from sinners; and it must also be the characteristic of all His followers.

Believer, the Lord Jesus has sanctified you through His own blood, and He desires to make you experience, through that blood, the full power of this sanctification. Endeavor to gain a clear impression of what has taken place in you through the sprinkling of that blood. The holy God desires to have you entirely for Himself. No one, nothing, may any longer have the least right over you; nor have you any right over yourself. God has separated you unto Himself, and so that you might feel this, He set His mark upon you. This mark is the most wonderful thing that is to be found on earth or in heaven—the blood of Jesus. The blood in which the life of the eternal Son of God is found, the blood that on the throne of grace is ever before God's face, the blood that assures you of full redemption from the power of sin—that blood is sprinkled upon you as a sign that you belong to God.

Believer, I urge you, let every thought about the blood awaken in you the glorious confession, "By His own blood, the Lord Jesus has sanctified me. He has taken complete possession of me for God, and I belong entirely to God."

We have seen that sanctification is more than separation. That is only the beginning. We have also seen that personal consecration, and hearty and willing surrender to live only for and in God's holy will, are part of sanctification.

In what way can the blood of Christ work out this surrender in us and sanctify us in that surrender? The answer is not difficult. It is not enough to believe in the power of the blood to redeem us and to free us from sin; we must, above all, notice the source of this power.

We know that it has this power because of the willingness with which the Lord Jesus surrendered Himself. In the shedding of His blood, He sanctified Himself, offered

Himself entirely to God and His holiness. It is because of this that the blood is so holy and possesses such sanctifying power. In the blood we have an impressive representation of the utter self-surrender of Christ. The blood ever speaks of the consecration of Jesus to the Father; it tells of the opening of the way to victory over sin, and it supplies the power for that victory. The closer we come into contact with the blood, and the more we live under the deep impression of having been sprinkled by the blood, we will hear more clearly the voice of the blood declaring, "Entire surrender to God is the way to full redemption from sin."

Consecration and surrender are also part of sanctification.

The voice of the blood will not speak simply to teach us or to awaken thought; the blood speaks with a divine and life-giving power. What it commands, it also bestows. It works out in us the same disposition that was in our Lord Jesus. By His own blood, Jesus sanctifies us so that we, holding nothing back, might surrender ourselves with all our hearts to the holy will of God.

But consecration itself, even along with and following separation, is still only a preparation. Entire sanctification takes place when God takes possession of and fills with His glory the temple that is consecrated to Him. *"There I will meet with the children of Israel, and the tabernacle shall be sanctified by my glory"* (Exodus 29:43). Actual, complete sanctification consists in God's impartation of His own holiness—of Himself.

Here, also, the blood speaks; it tells us that heaven is opened, that the powers of the heavenly life have come down to earth, that every hindrance has been removed. God can make His abode with man.

Immediate nearness and fellowship with God are made possible by the blood of Jesus. The believer who surrenders himself unreservedly to the blood obtains the full assurance that God will bestow Himself wholly and will reveal His holiness in him.

How glorious are the results of such a sanctification! Through the Holy Spirit, the soul's intimacy is in the living experience of God's abiding nearness, accompanied by the awakening of the tenderest carefulness against sin, guarded by caution and the fear of God.

But to live in watchfulness against sin does not satisfy the soul. The temple must not only be cleansed; it must also be filled with God's glory. All the virtues of divine holiness, as manifested in the Lord Jesus, are to be sought and found in fellowship with God. Sanctification means union with God, fellowship in His will, sharing His life, conformity to His image.

Christians, *"Jesus also, that he might sanctify the people with his own blood, suffered without the gate. Let us go forth therefore unto him without the camp, bearing his reproach"* (Hebrews 13:12–13). Yes, it is He who sanctifies His people. *"Let us go forth...unto him"* (verse 13). Let us trust Him to make known to us the power of the blood. Let us yield ourselves wholly to its blessed power. This blood, through which He sanctified Himself, has entered heaven to open it for us. It can make our hearts also a throne of God so that the grace and glory of God may dwell in us. Yes, *"let us go forth...unto him without the camp"* (verse 13). He who is willing to lose and say farewell to everything, in order that Jesus may sanctify him, will not fail to obtain the blessing. He who is willing at any cost to experience the full power of the precious blood can confidently know that he will be sanctified by Jesus Himself, through that blood.

"And the very God of peace sanctify you wholly" (1 Thessalonians 5:23). Amen.

six

Cleansed by the Blood
to Serve the Living God

six

Cleansed by the Blood to Serve the Living God

Now in Christ Jesus ye who sometimes were far off are made nigh by the blood of Christ.
—Ephesians 2:13

How much more shall the blood of Christ...purge your conscience...to serve the living God?
—Hebrews 9:14

After our study of sanctification through the blood, we will now consider the intimate relationship with God into which we are introduced by sanctification.

Sanctification and intimacy are closely related facts in Scripture. Apart from sanctification there can be no such relationship. How could one who is unholy have fellowship with a holy God? On the other hand, without this relationship there can be no growth in holiness; it is always and only in fellowship with the Holy One that holiness can be found.

The intimate connection between sanctification and relationship appears plainly in the story of the revolt of Nadab and Abihu. God made this the occasion of a clear statement concerning the distinctive nature of the priesthood in Israel. He said, *"I will be sanctified in them that come nigh me"* (Leviticus 10:3). Then again, in the conspiracy of Korah against Moses and Aaron, Moses, speaking for God said, *"Even to morrow the LORD will show who are his, and who is holy; and will cause him to come near unto him: even him whom he hath chosen will he cause to come near unto him"* (Numbers 16:5).

We have already seen that God's election and separation of His own unto Himself are closely bound up with sanctification. It is evident here, also, that the glory and blessing secured by this election to holiness is nothing else than intimacy with God. This is indeed the highest and one perfect blessing for man, who was created for God and to enjoy His love. The psalmist sang, *"Blessed is the man whom thou choosest, and causest to approach unto thee, that he may dwell in thy courts"* (Psalm 65:4). In the nature of the case, consecration to God and nearness to Him are the same thing.

The highest blessing for man is intimacy with God.

The sprinkling of the blood, which sanctifies man unto God and takes possession of him for God, bestows at the same time the right of intimacy.

It was thus with the priests in Israel. In the record of their consecration we read, *"And* [Moses] *brought Aaron's sons, and Moses put of the blood upon the tip of their right ear, and upon the thumbs of their right hands"*

(Leviticus 8:24). Those who belong to God may, and indeed must, live in nearness to Him; they belong to Him. This is illustrated in the case of our Lord, our great High Priest, who *"by his own blood...entered once into the holy place"* (Hebrews 9:12).

It is the same with every believer, according to the Word: *"Having therefore, brethren, boldness to enter into the holiest by the blood of Jesus,...let us draw near..., having our hearts sprinkled from an evil conscience"* (Hebrews 10:19, 22). The word *"enter,"* as used in this verse, is the word used of the approach of the priest to God. In the same way, in the book of Revelation, our right to draw near as priests is declared to be by the power of the blood. We were *"washed...from our sins in his own blood"*—the blood of Him who *"hath made us kings and priests unto God and his Father; to him be glory and dominion for ever and ever"* (Revelation 1:5–6). *"These are they which...washed their robes, and made them white in the blood of the Lamb. Therefore are they before the throne of God, and serve him day and night in his temple"* (Revelation 7:14–15).

One of the most glorious blessings made possible for us by the power of the blood is that of drawing near the throne into the very presence of God. So that we may understand what this blessing means, let us consider what is contained in it. It includes:

- First, the right to dwell in the presence of God
- Second, the duty of offering spiritual sacrifices to God
- Third, the power to procure blessing for others

Cleansed by the Blood to Serve the Living God

The Right to Dwell in the Presence of God

Although this privilege belonged exclusively to the priests in Israel, we know that *they* had free access to the dwelling place of God. They had to abide there continually. As members of the household of God, they ate the show-bread and partook of the sacrifices. A true Israelite thought there was no higher privilege than this. It was thus expressed by the psalmist, *"Blessed* [happy] *is the man whom thou choosest, and causest to approach unto thee, that he may dwell in thy courts: we shall be satisfied with the goodness of thy house, even of thy holy temple"* (Psalm 65:4).

The blood of Christ has opened the way to God's presence.

It was because of the manifested presence of God there that believers, in those old days, longed for the house of God with such strong desire. The cry was, *"When shall I come and appear before God?"* (Psalm 42:2). They understood something of the spiritual meaning of the privilege of drawing near to God. It represented to them the enjoyment of His love, His fellowship, His protection, and His blessing. They could exclaim, *"Oh how great is thy goodness, which thou hast laid up for them that fear thee....Thou shalt hide them in the secret of thy presence"* (Psalm 31:19–20).

The precious blood of Christ has opened the way for the believer into God's presence, and intimacy with Him is a deep, spiritual reality. He who knows the full power of the blood is brought so near that he can always live in the immediate presence of God and in the enjoyment of the unspeakable blessings attached to it. There, the child of God has the assurance of God's love; he experiences and enjoys it. God Himself imparts it. He lives daily in the friendship and fellowship of God. As God's child, he makes his thoughts and wishes known to the Father, with perfect freedom. In this intimacy with God, he possesses all that he needs; he lacks *"no good thing"* (Psalm 84:11). His soul is kept in perfect rest and peace, because God is with him (Isaiah 26:3). He receives all necessary direction and teaching. God's eye is ever upon him, guiding him. In intimacy with God, he is able to hear the softest whispers of the Holy Spirit. He learns to understand the slightest sign of his Father's will and to follow it. His strength continually increases, for God is his strength, and God is ever with him.

In intimacy with God, we possess all that we need.

Fellowship with God has a wonderful influence on his life and character. The presence of God fills him with humility, fear, and a holy circumspection. He lives as in the presence of a king. Fellowship with God produces God-like inclinations in him. Beholding the image of God, he is changed into the same image (2 Corinthians 3:18). Dwelling with the Holy One makes him holy. He can say, *"It is good for me to draw near to God"* (Psalm 73:28).

Oh, you who are the children of the new covenant, do you not have a thousand times more reasons to speak in the same way, now that the veil has been torn asunder and the way opened for living always in God's holy presence? May this high privilege awaken our desires. Intimacy with God, fellowship with God, dwelling with God and He with us—may it become impossible for us to be satisfied with anything less. This is the true Christian life.

But relationship with God is not only so blessed because of the salvation enjoyed in it but also on account of the service that may be rendered because of that intimacy. Let us, therefore, consider the spiritual sacrifices that we may offer to God.

The Duty of Offering Spiritual Sacrifices to God

Our duty to bring spiritual sacrifices to God is a further privilege. The enjoyment of the priests in drawing near to God in His dwelling place was subordinated entirely to something higher. They were there as servants of the Holy Place; to bring to God, in His house, that which belonged to Him. Only as they found joy, in drawing near to God, could that service become truly blessed.

The service consisted in the bringing in of the blood of sprinkling; the preparation of the incense to fill the house with its fragrance; and, further, the ordering of everything that pertained, according to God's Word, to the arrangement of His house.

Their duty was to so guard and serve and provide for the dwelling place of the Most High that it would be worthy of Him and of His glory, and that His good pleasure in it might be fulfilled.

If the blood of Jesus brings us near, it is also, chiefly, so that we will live before God as His servants and bring to Him the spiritual sacrifices that are well-pleasing in His sight.

The priests brought the blood into the Holy Place before God. In our relationship with God, there is no offering that we can bring more pleasing to Him than a believing honoring of the blood of the Lamb. Every act of humble trust or of hearty thanksgiving, in which we direct the attention of the Father to the blood and speak its praises, is acceptable to Him. Our whole abiding there, and our intimacy, from hour to hour must be a glorifying of the blood before God.

The priests brought the incense into the Holy Place so as to fill God's house with fragrance. The prayers of God's people are the delightful incense with which He desires to be surrounded in His habitation. The value of prayer does not consist merely in its being the means of obtaining things we need. No! It has a higher aim than that. It is a ministry of God in which He delights.

Our duty to bring spiritual sacrifices is a privilege.

The life of a believer who truly enjoys drawing near to God through the blood is a life of unceasing prayer. In a deep sense of dependence—for each moment, for each step—grace is sought and expected. In the blessed conviction of God's nearness and unchanging goodness, the soul pours itself out in the confident assurance of faith that every promise will be fulfilled. In the midst of the joy that the light of God's face bestows, thanksgiving and adoration arise along with prayer.

Cleansed by the Blood to Serve the Living God

These are the spiritual offerings—the offerings of the lips of the priests of God—continually presented to Him. They have been sanctified and brought near by the blood so that they might ever live and walk in His presence.

But there is still something more. It was the duty of the priests to attend to everything for cleansing or provision that was necessary in the ministry of the house. What is the ministry now, under the new covenant? Thanks be to God, there are no outward or exclusive arrangements for divine worship. No! The Father has so ordered that whatever anyone does who is walking in His presence, just because of this fact, presents a spiritual offering to God. Everything the believer does—if only he does it as in God's presence and as a service to God—it is a priestly sacrifice, well-pleasing to God. *"Whether therefore ye eat, or drink, or whatsoever ye do, do all to the glory of God"* (1 Corinthians 10:31). *"Whatsoever ye do in word or deed, do all in the name of the Lord Jesus, giving thanks to God and the Father by him"* (Colossians 3:17). In this way, all our actions become thank-offerings to God.

In the midst of God's presence, thanksgiving and adoration arise along with our prayers.

How little Christians recognize the glory of a life of complete consecration, to be spent always in intimacy with God!

Because I am cleansed, sanctified, and brought near by the power of the blood, my earthly calling, my whole life, even my eating and drinking are a spiritual service. My work, my business, my money, my house, and everything with which I have dealings become sanctified by the presence of God because I walk in His presence. The poorest earthly work is a priestly service when it is performed by a priest of God's temple.

But even this does not exhaust the glory of the blessing of intimacy. The highest blessing of the priesthood is that the priest appears as the representative of others before God.

The Power to Procure Blessing for Others

This is what gives full glory to nearness to God.

In Israel the priests were the mediators between God and the people. They carried into the presence of God the sins and needs of the people; they obtained from God the power to declare the pardon of sin and the right of blessing the people.

> My work, my business, my money, my house become sanctified by the presence of God because I walk in His presence.

This privilege now belongs to all believers, as the priestly family of the new covenant. When God permitted His redeemed ones to approach Him through the blood, it was so that He might bless them in order that they might become a blessing to others. Priestly mediation; a priestly heart that can have the needed sympathy with those who are weak; a priestly power to obtain the blessing of God in the temple and convey it to others—in these things, intimacy, or the drawing near to God through the blood, manifests its highest power and glory.

We can exercise our priestly dignity in a twofold manner: first, through intercession, and second, in the form of instruments.

By Intercession

The ministry of intercession is one of the highest privileges of the child of God. It does not mean that in this ministry we, having ascertained that there is a need in the world or in some particular person, pour out our wishes in prayer to God, asking for the necessary supply. That is good, so far as it goes, and it brings a blessing with it. But the ministry of intercession is something more wonderful than that and finds its power in *"the prayer of faith"* (James 5:15). This *"prayer of faith"* is a different thing than the outpouring of our wishes to God, and leaving them with Him.

The ministry of intercession is one of the highest privileges of the child of God.

In the true *"prayer of faith,"* the intercessor must spend time with God to take hold of the promises of His Word, and he must permit himself to be taught by the Holy Spirit whether the promises can be applied to this particular case. He takes upon himself, as a burden, the sin and need that are the subject of prayer. He then lays hold of the promise concerning it, as though it were for himself. He remains in the presence of God, until God, by His Spirit, awakens the faith that, in this matter, the prayer has been heard. In this way, parents sometimes pray for their children, ministers for their congregations, laborers in God's vineyard for the souls committed to them, until they know that their prayer is heard. It is the blood that, by its power of bringing us near to God, bestows such wonderful liberty to pray until the answer is obtained.

Oh, if we understood more perfectly what it really means to dwell in the presence of God, we would manifest more power in the exercise of our holy priesthood!

As Instruments

A further manifestation of our priestly mediation is that we not only obtain some blessing for others by intercession, but we become the instruments by whom it is ministered. Every believer is called and feels himself compelled by love to labor on behalf of others. He knows that God has blessed him so that he might be a blessing to others, yet the complaint is generally that believers have no power for this work of bringing blessing to others. They are not, they say, in a condition to exercise an influence over others by their words.

If they will not dwell in the sanctuary, this is no surprise. We read that *"the Lord separated the tribe of Levi... to stand before the Lord to minister unto him, and to bless in his name"* (Deuteronomy 10:8). The priestly power of blessing depends on the priestlike life in the presence of God. He who there experiences the power of the blood to preserve him, the helpless one, will have courage to believe that the blood can really deliver others. The holy life-giving power of the blood will create in him the same disposition as that in which Jesus shed it—the sacrifice of himself to redeem others.

In intimacy with God, our love will be set on fire by the love of God; our belief that God will surely make use of us will be strengthened; the Spirit of Jesus will take possession of us to enable us to labor in humility, in wisdom, and in power; and our weakness and poverty will become the vessels in which God's power can work. From our words and examples, blessing will flow because we dwell with Him who is pure blessing, and He will not permit anyone to be near Him without also being filled with His blessing.

> In intimacy with God, our love will be set on fire by the love of God.

Beloved, is not the life prepared for us a glorious and a blessed one: the enjoyment of the blessedness of being near to God; the carrying out of the ministry of His house; the imparting of His blessing to others?

Let no one think that the full blessing is not for him, that such a life is too high for him. In the power of Jesus' blood, we have the assurance that this drawing near is also for us if only we wholly yield ourselves to it.

For those who truly desire this blessing, I give the following advice. Remember that this, and nothing less, is designed for you. All of us who are God's children have been brought near by the blood. All of us can desire the full experience of it. Let us only hold fast to this: "The life of intimacy with God is for me." The Father does not wish that one of His children should be far off. We cannot please our God as we ought if we live without this blessing. We are priests; grace to live as priests is prepared for us; free entrance into the sanctuary as our abiding place is for us. We can be assured of this: As His children, we have been given God's indwelling holy presence as our right. Let us lay hold of this.

Seek to make the full power of the blood your own possession in all its blessed effects. It is in the power of the blood that relationship is possible. Let your heart be filled with faith in the power of the blood of reconciliation. Sin has been so entirely atoned for and blotted out that its power to keep you away from God has been completely, and forever, taken away. Live in the joyful knowledge that sin is powerless to separate you one moment from God. Believe that, by the blood, you have been fully justified, and thus you have a righteous claim to a place in the sanctuary. Let the blood also cleanse you. From the fellowship that follows, you can expect the inner deliverance from the defilement of sin that still dwells in you. Say with the Scriptures, *"How much more shall the blood of Christ...purge your conscience...to serve the living God?"* Let the blood sanctify you, separate you for God in undivided consecration, to be filled by Him. Let the pardoning, cleansing, sanctifying power of the blood have free course in you. You will discover how this brings you, as it were, automatically near to God and protects you.

Do not fear to expect that Jesus Himself will reveal in you the power of the blood to bring you near to God. The blood was shed to unite us to God. The blood has accomplished its work and will perfect it in you. The blood has unspeakable virtue and glory in God's sight.

The mercy seat sprinkled with blood is the chosen place of God's abode and His throne of grace. He draws near with joy and good pleasure to the heart that surrenders itself entirely to the effectiveness of the blood.

The blood has irresistible power. Through the blood, Jesus was raised up from the grave and carried into heaven. Be assured that the blood is able to preserve you every day in God's presence by its divine life-giving power.

As precious and all-powerful as the blood is, so sure and certain is your abiding with God, if only your trust is steadfast.

The blood has irresistible power.

"Washed...and made...white in the blood of the Lamb. Therefore they are before the throne of God, and serve Him day and night in His temple" (Revelation 7:14–15). This word about the eternal glory also has a bearing upon our lives on earth. The fuller our faith and experience of the power of the blood, the closer the intimacy; the surer our abiding near the throne, the wider the entrance to the unbroken ministry of God in His sanctuary; and here on earth, the greater the power to serve the living God, the richer the priestly blessing that you will spread around you. O Lord, may this word have its full power over us now, here, and hereafter!

seven
Dwelling in *"The Holiest"* through the Blood

Dwelling in *"The Holiest"* through the Blood

Having therefore, brethren, boldness to enter into the holiest by the blood of Jesus, by a new and living way, which he hath consecrated for us, through the veil, that is to say, his flesh; and having an high priest over the house of God; let us draw near with a true heart in full assurance of faith, having our hearts sprinkled from an evil conscience, and our bodies washed with pure water.
—Hebrews 10:19–22

In the words of this Scripture passage, we have a summary of the chief contents of this epistle and of the good news about God's grace, as the Holy Spirit caused it to be presented to the Hebrews and also to us.

Through sin, man was driven out of Eden, away from the presence and fellowship of God. God, in His mercy, sought from the beginning to restore the broken fellowship.

To this end, He gave to Israel, through the shadowy types of the tabernacle, the expectation of a time to come, when the wall of partition would be removed so that His people might dwell in His presence. *"When shall I come and appear before God?"* (Psalm 42:2) was the longing sigh of the believers of the old covenant.

It is also the sigh of many of God's children under the new covenant who do not understand that the way into the Holiest has really been opened, and that every child of God may, and ought, to have his real dwelling place there.

Oh, my brothers and sisters who long to experience the full power of the redemption that Jesus has accomplished, come with me to hear what our God says to us about the opened Holy Place and the freedom with which we can enter through the blood.

Every child of God may, and ought, to dwell in the Holiest.

The passage at the beginning of this chapter shows us in a first series of four words what God has prepared for us, as the sure ground on which our fellowship with Him may rest. Then, in a second series of four words that follow, we learn how we may be prepared to enter into that fellowship and to live in it.

Read the text with attention, and you will see that the words *"let us draw near"* are the center of it all. Let us consider the following:

- First, what God has prepared for us
- Second, how God prepares us for what He has prepared for us
- Finally, *"let us draw near"*

The Power of the Blood of Christ

Having therefore, brethren, boldness to enter into the holiest by the blood of Jesus, by a new and living way, which he hath consecrated for us, through the veil, that is to say, his flesh; and having an high priest over the house of God; let us draw near with a true heart in full assurance of faith, having our hearts sprinkled from an evil conscience, and our bodies washed with pure water.

What God Has Prepared for Us

The Holiest

"Having...boldness to enter into the holiest..., let us draw near."

To bring us into the Holiest is the end of the redemptive work of Jesus, and he who does not know what the Holiest is cannot enjoy the full benefit of redemption.

What is this Holiest? It is just the place where God dwells: the Holiest, the dwelling place of the Most High. This does not refer only to heaven but to the holiest spiritual place of God's presence.

Under the old covenant there was a material sanctuary (Hebrews 8:2; 9:1), the dwelling place of God, in which the priests dwelt in God's presence and served Him. Under the new covenant, there is the true spiritual tabernacle, not confined to any place; this is the Holiest, where God reveals Himself (John 4:23–25).

What a glorious privilege it is to enter into the Holiest and dwell there, to walk all day long in the presence of God. What a rich blessing is poured out there. In the Holiest, the favor and fellowship of God are enjoyed, the life and blessing of God are experienced, the power and joy of God are found. Life is spent in the Holiest in priestly purity and consecration; there, the incense of sweet savor is burned, and sacrifices acceptable to God are offered. It is a holy life of prayer and blessedness.

Under the old covenant, everything was material; the sanctuary was also material. Under the new covenant, everything is spiritual; the true sanctuary owes its existence to the power of the Holy Spirit. Through the Holy Spirit, a real life in the Holiest is possible, and the knowledge that God walks there can be as certain as in the case of the priests of old. The Spirit makes the work that Jesus has accomplished real in our experience.

What a glorious privilege it is to enter into the Holiest and dwell there.

Believer in Jesus Christ, do you have liberty to enter into and abide in the Holiest? As one who has been redeemed, it is a fitting thing for you to make your home there, and not elsewhere, for Christ cannot elsewhere reveal the full power of His redemption. But there, He can bless you richly. Understand it, then, and let the purpose of God and of our Lord Jesus be yours also. May it be the one desire of our hearts to enter into the Holiest, to live in the Holiest, to minister in the Holiest. We can confidently expect the Holy Spirit to give us a right idea of the glory of entering into a dwelling in the Holiest.

Liberty through the Blood

Admission to the Holiest, like the Holiest itself, belongs to God. God Himself thought of it and prepared it; we have the liberty, the freedom, the right to enter by the blood of Jesus. The blood of Jesus exercises such a wonderful power that, through it, a son of perdition may obtain full freedom to enter into the divine sanctuary, the Holiest. *"Ye who sometimes were far off are made nigh by the blood of Christ"* (Ephesians 2:13).

And how does the blood exercise this wonderful power? Scripture says, *"The life...is in the blood"* (Leviticus 17:11). The power of the blood is in the worth of the life. In the blood of Jesus, the power of the divine life dwelt and worked; in Him, the blood already has almighty and unceasing power.

The power of the blood has opened heaven.

But that power could not be exercised for reconciliation until it was first shed. By bearing the punishment of sin unto death, the Lord Jesus conquered the power of sin and brought it to nothing. *"The strength of sin is the law"* (1 Corinthians 15:56). By perfectly fulfilling the law when He shed His blood under its curse, His blood has made sin entirely powerless. So the blood has its wonderful power, not only because the life of God's Son was in it but also because it was given as an atonement for sin. This is the reason Scripture speaks so highly about the blood. Through the blood of the everlasting covenant, God has brought our Lord Jesus from the dead (Hebrews 13:20).

Through His own blood, He has entered into the Holiest (Hebrews 9:12). The power of the blood has entirely destroyed the power of sin, death, the grave, and hell so that our Surety could go out from hell. The power of the blood has opened heaven so that our Surety could freely enter its blessedness.

And now, we also have liberty to enter through the blood. Sin took away our liberty of approach to God; the blood perfectly restores this liberty to us. He who will take time to meditate on the power of that blood, taking hold of it believingly for himself, will obtain a wonderful view of the liberty and directness with which we can now have intimacy with God.

We now have liberty to enter through the blood.

Oh, the divine, wonderful power of the blood! Through the blood, we enter into the Holiest. The blood pleads for us, and in us, with an eternal, ceaseless effect. It removes sin from God's sight and from our consciences. Every moment we have free, full entrance, and we can have intimacy with God through the blood.

Oh, that the Holy Spirit might reveal to us the full power of the blood! Under His teaching, we enjoy a full entrance to intimate fellowship with the Father. Our life is in the Holiest through the blood.

"A New and Living Way"

"Having therefore, brethren, boldness to enter into the holiest by the blood of Jesus, by a new and living way, which he hath consecrated for us, through the veil, that is to say, his flesh." The blood bestows our right of entrance. The way, as a living and life-giving one, bestows the power. That He has consecrated this way by His flesh does not

mean that this is merely a different way of saying, *"Through His blood"* (Ephesians 1:7; Colossians 1:14). By no means.

Jesus has shed His blood for us; in this particular action, we cannot follow Him. But the way by which He walked when He shed His blood—the tearing of the veil of His flesh—in that way, we must follow Him. What He did by opening that way is a living power that draws and carries us as we enter the Holiest. The lesson we have to learn here is this: The way into the Holiest is through the torn veil of the flesh.

We must follow Jesus in the way He walked.

It was so with Jesus. The veil that separated God and us was the flesh. Sin has its power in the flesh, and only through the taking away of sin may the veil be removed. When Jesus came in the flesh, He could tear the veil only by dying. Therefore, in order to bring to nothing the power of the flesh and sin, He offered up the flesh and delivered it to death. This is what gave worth and power to the shedding of His blood.

And this now remains as the law for each one who desires to enter the Holiest through His blood: It must be through the torn veil of the flesh. The blood demands, the blood accomplishes, the tearing of the flesh. Where the blood of Jesus works powerfully, there always follows the putting to death of the flesh. He who desires to spare the flesh cannot enter into the Holiest. The flesh must be sacrificed, given over to death. To the extent that the believer perceives the sinfulness of his flesh and puts to death all that is in the flesh, he will better understand the power of the blood. The believer does not do this in his own strength; he comes by a living way that Jesus has consecrated. The life-giving power of Jesus works in this way. The Christian is crucified and dead with Jesus: *"They that are Christ's have crucified the flesh"* (Galatians 5:24). It is in fellowship with Christ that we enter through the veil.

Where the blood of Jesus works, there always follows the putting to death of the flesh.

Oh, glorious way, the *"new and living way,"* full of life-giving power, that Christ has *"consecrated for us"*! By this way, we have the liberty to enter into the Holiest by the blood of Jesus. May the Lord God lead us along this way, through the torn veil, through the death of the flesh, to the full life of the Spirit. Then, we will find our dwelling place within the veil, in the Holiest with God. Each sacrifice of the flesh leads us, through the blood, further into the Holiest.*

The Great Priest

"Having an high priest over the house of God; let us draw near."

Praised be God, we have not only the work but also the living person of Christ as we enter the Holiest; not

---

* Author's Note: Compare further, with care, 1 Peter 3:18, *"Christ...[was] put to death in the flesh"*; 1 Peter 4:1, *"Christ suffered for us in the flesh"*; and Romans 8:3, *"God...condemned sin in the flesh."*

only the blood and the living way but also Jesus Himself, as *"high priest over the house of God."*

The priests who went into the earthly sanctuary could do so only because of their relationship to the high priest; none but the sons of Aaron were priests. We have an entrance into the Holiest because of our relationship to the Lord Jesus. He said to the Father, *"Behold, I and the children whom the LORD hath given me"* (Isaiah 8:18).

He is the great Priest. The epistle to the Hebrews has shown us that He is the true Melchizedek, the eternal Son, who has an eternal and changeless priesthood, and as Priest is seated on the throne. He lives there to pray always; *"wherefore he is able also to save them to the uttermost that come unto God by him"* (Hebrews 7:25), a great and all-powerful Priest.

Jesus is the great Priest.

"An high priest over the house of God," He is appointed over the entire ministry of the Holiest, of the house of God. All the people of God are under His care. If we desire to enter the Holiest, He is there to receive us and to present us to the Father. He Himself will complete in us the sprinkling of the blood. Through the blood, He has entered; through the blood, He also brings us in. He will teach us all the duties of the Holiest and of our responsibilities there. He makes our prayers acceptable, as well as our offerings and the duties of our ministry, however weak they are. Moreover, He bestows on us heavenly light and heavenly power for our work and our lives in

the Holiest. It is He who imparts the life and the Spirit of the Holiest. Just as His blood procured an entrance, His sacrifice of His flesh is the *"living way."* As we enter, it is He by whom we are kept abiding there and always are able to walk in a way that is well-pleasing to God. As the sympathetic High Priest, He knows how to stoop to each one, even the weakest. Yes, this is what makes intimacy with God in the Holiest so attractive: We find Jesus there, as a *"high priest over the house of God."*

Let us draw near!

And just when it seems to us as if the Holiest is too high or too holy for us, and that we cannot understand what the power of the blood is, and how we are to walk in the *"new and living way,"* then we may look up to the living Savior Himself to teach us and to bring us Himself into the Holiest. He is the *"priest over the house of God."* You have only to cling to Him and you will be in the Holiest.

"Let us draw near," seeing that we have the Holiest where God waits for us, the blood that gives us liberty, the living way that carries us, and the High Priest to help us. *"Let us draw near."* Yes, *"let us draw near."* Let nothing hold us back from making use of these wonderful blessings that God has designed for us. It is into the Holiest that we are to enter; our right has been obtained for us by the blood of Jesus; by His own footsteps, He has consecrated the way. He lives in His eternal priesthood to receive us in the Holiest, to sanctify, to preserve, to

bless us. Oh, let us no longer hesitate or turn back. Let us sacrifice all for this one thing; in view of what God has prepared for us, *"let us draw near"* by the hand of Jesus to appear before our Father and to find our life in the light of His countenance.

And do we desire to know how we can now be prepared to enter? Our text gives us a glorious answer to this question.

How We Are Prepared

Draw Near with a True Heart

"With a true heart"—this is the second series of four words, which tells us how we are prepared. This is the first of the four demands made on the believer who wishes to *"draw near."* It is coupled with the second demand, *"in full assurance of faith,"* and it is chiefly in its union with the second demand that we correctly understand what *"a true heart"* means.

The preaching of the gospel always begins with repentance and faith. Man cannot receive God's grace by faith if, at the same time, sin is not forsaken. In the progress of the life of faith, this law is always binding. The *"full assurance of faith"* cannot be reached without *"a true heart,"* a heart that is wholly honest with God, that is surrendered entirely to Him. The Holiest cannot be entered without *"a true heart,"* a heart that is truly desirous of seeking what it claims to seek.

"Let us draw near with a true heart"—a heart that truly desires to forsake everything to dwell in the Holiest, and forsaking everything, to possess God; a heart

that truly abandons everything in order to yield itself to the authority and power of the blood; a heart that truly chooses the *"new and living way"* in order to go through the veil with Christ by the tearing of the flesh; a heart that truly and entirely gives itself to the indwelling and lordship of Jesus.

"Let us draw near with a true heart." Without a true heart, there is no entrance into the Holiest.

But who has a true heart? The new heart that God has given is *"a true heart."* Recognize this. By the power of the Spirit of God who dwells in that new heart, place yourself, by an exercise of your will, on the side of God against the sin that is still in your flesh. Say to the Lord Jesus, the High Priest, that you submit and cast down before Him every sin and all of your self-life, forsaking all to follow Him.

The preaching of the gospel always begins with repentance and faith.

And regarding the hidden depths of sin in your flesh, of which you are not yet conscious, and the malice of your heart—for them provision is also made. *"Search me, O God, and know my heart"* (Psalm 139:23). Subject yourself continually to the heart-searching light of the Spirit. He will uncover what is hidden from you. He who does this has *"a true heart"* to enter into the Holiest.

Let us not be afraid to say to God that we *"draw near with a true heart."* Let us be assured that God will not judge us according to the perfection of what we do but according to the honesty with which we yield ourselves to lay aside every known sin, and with which we accept conviction by the Holy Spirit of all our hidden sin. A heart that does this honestly is, in God's sight, *"a true heart."* And with *"a true heart,"* the Holiest is approached through the blood. Praised be God! Through His Spirit, we have *"a true heart."*

In Full Assurance of Faith

We know what place faith occupies in God's dealings with man. *"Without faith it is impossible to please him"* (Hebrews 11:6). Here, at the entrance into the Holiest, all depends on the *"full assurance of faith."*

There must be a *"full assurance of faith"* that there is a Holy Place where we can dwell and walk with God; that the power of the precious blood has conquered sin so perfectly that nothing can prevent our undisturbed fellowship with God; that the way that Jesus has sanctified through His flesh is a living way, which carries those who tread on it with eternal living power; that the great *"high priest over the house of God"* can *"save them to the uttermost that come unto God by him"* (Hebrews 7:25); and that He by His Spirit, works in us everything that is necessary for life in the Holiest. These things we must believe and hold fast in the *"full assurance of faith."*

But how can I get there? How can my faith grow to this full assurance? By fellowship with *"Jesus the author and finisher of our faith"* (Hebrews 12:2). As the great *"priest over the house of God,"* He enables us to take hold of faith. By considering Him, His wonderful love,

His perfect work, His precious and all-powerful blood, faith is sustained and strengthened. God has given Him to awaken faith. By keeping our eyes fixed on Him, faith and the *"full assurance of faith"* become ours.

In handling the Word of God, remember that *"faith cometh by hearing, and hearing by the word of God"* (Romans 10:17). Faith comes by the Word and grows by the Word, but not the Word as letter, but as the voice of Jesus. Only *"the words that I speak unto you, they are spirit, and they are life"* (John 6:63); only in Him are the promises of God *"yea, and...Amen"* (2 Corinthians 1:20). Take time to meditate on the Word and treasure it in your heart, but always with a heart set on Jesus Himself. It is faith in Jesus that saves. The Word that is taken to Jesus in prayer and talked over with Him is the Word that is effective.

Through His Spirit, we have *"a true heart."*

Remember that *"whosoever hath, to him shall be given"* (Matthew 13:12). Make use of the faith that you have; exercise it, declare it, and let your believing trust in God become the chief occupation of your life. God wishes to have children who believe Him; He desires nothing so much as faith. Get accustomed to say with each prayer, "Lord I believe that I will obtain this." As you read each promise in Scripture, say, "Lord, I believe You will fulfill this in me." The whole day through, make it your holy habit in everything—yes, in everything—to exercise trust in God's guidance and God's blessing.

The Power of the Blood of Christ

To enter into the Holiest, *"full assurance of faith"* is necessary. *"Let us draw near...in full assurance of faith."* Redemption through the blood is so perfect and powerful; the love and grace of Jesus so overflowing; the blessedness of dwelling in the Holiest is so surely for us and within our reach—*"let us draw near...in full assurance of faith."*

With Our Hearts Cleansed

"Let us draw near..., having our hearts sprinkled [cleansed] *from an evil conscience."*

The heart is the center of human life.

The heart is the center of human life, and the conscience is the center of the heart. By his conscience, a person realizes his relationship to God; and an evil conscience tells him that all is not right between God and himself—not merely that he commits sin but that he is sinful and alienated from God. A good or clear conscience bears witness that he is well-pleasing to God (Hebrews 11:5). It bears witness not only that his sins are forgiven but also that his heart is sincere before God. He who desires to enter the Holiest must have his heart cleansed from an evil conscience. The words are translated *"our hearts sprinkled from an evil conscience."* It is the sprinkling of the blood that avails. The blood of Christ will purify your conscience to serve the living God.

We have already seen that entrance to the Holiest is by the blood, by which Jesus went to the Father. But that is not enough. There is a twofold sprinkling: The priests who drew near to God were not only reconciled through the sprinkling of blood before God on the altar, but their very persons also had to be sprinkled with the blood. The blood of Jesus must be brought by the Holy Spirit into direct contact with our hearts so that our hearts become cleansed from an evil conscience. The blood removes all self-condemnation. It cleanses the conscience. Conscience then witnesses that the removal of guilt has been so perfectly completed that there is no longer the least separation between God and us. Conscience bears witness that we are well-pleasing to God; that our hearts are cleansed; that we, through the sprinkling of the blood, are in true living fellowship with God. Yes, the blood of Jesus Christ cleanses from all sin, not only from the guilt but also from the stain of sin.

Through the power of the blood, our fallen nature is prevented from exercising its power. Just as a fountain by its gentle spray cleanses the grass that otherwise would be covered with dust and keeps it fresh and green, so the blood works with ceaseless effect to keep the soul clean. A heart that lives under the full power of the blood is a clean heart, cleansed from a guilty conscience, prepared to *"draw near"* with perfect freedom. The whole heart, the whole inner being, is cleansed by a divine operation.

The blood removes all self-condemnation.

"Let us draw near..., having our hearts sprinkled from an evil conscience." Let us *"in full assurance of faith"* believe that our hearts are cleansed. Let us honor the blood greatly by confessing before God that it cleanses us. The High Priest will, by His Holy Spirit, make us understand the

full meaning and power of having the heart cleansed by the blood, having the entrance to the Holy Place prepared through the blood, and having our hearts prepared by the blood for entrance. Having the heart cleansed, how glorious, then, it is to enter into and to abide in the Holiest!

With the Body Washed

"Let us draw near..., having...our bodies washed with pure water."

We belong to two worlds: The seen and the unseen. We have an inner, hidden life that brings us into touch with God, and an outer, bodily life by which we are in relationship with mankind. If this Scripture refers to the body, it refers to the entire life in the body, with all its activities.

The heart must be sprinkled with blood; the body must be washed with pure water. When the priests were consecrated, they were washed with water as well as sprinkled with blood (Exodus 29:4, 20–21). And if they went into the Holy Place, there was not only the altar with its blood but also the laver with its water. Christ, likewise, came *"by water and blood"* (1 John 5:6). He had His baptism with water and later with blood (Luke 12:50).

For us, there is also a twofold cleansing with water and blood. Baptism with water is for repentance, for laying aside of sin. *"Be baptized, and wash away thy sins"* (Acts 22:16). While the blood cleanses the heart, the inner man, baptism is the yielding of the body, with all its visible life, to separation from sin.

So *"let us draw near..., having our hearts sprinkled from an evil conscience, and our bodies washed with pure water."* The power of the blood to cleanse inwardly cannot be experienced unless we also cleanse ourselves from all filthiness of the flesh. The divine work of cleansing by the sprinkling of blood and the human work of cleansing by laying aside sin are inseparable.

We belong to two worlds: the seen and the unseen.

We must be clean to enter into the Holiest. Just as you would never dream of entering into the presence of a king unwashed, so you cannot imagine that you could come into the presence of God, in the Holy Place, if you are not cleansed from every sin. In the blood of Christ that cleanses from all sin, God has bestowed on you the power to cleanse yourself. Your desire to live with God in the Holiest must always be united with the most careful laying aside of even the least sin. The unclean may not enter the Holiest.

Praised be God, He desires to have us there. As His priests, we must minister to Him there. He desires our purity so that we may enjoy the blessing of the Holiest—that is, His holy fellowship. And He has taken care that, through the blood and by the Spirit, we may be clean.

"Let us draw near..., having our hearts sprinkled from an evil conscience, and our bodies washed with pure water."

"Let Us Draw Near"

The Holiest is open even for those in our congregations who have not yet truly turned to the Lord. For them, the sanctuary has been opened. The precious blood, the living way, and the High Priest are for them. With great confidence, we dare to invite even them. *"Let us draw near."* Oh, do not despise it, my friends still far from God; oh, despise no longer God's wonderful grace. Draw near to the Father who has so earnestly sent this invitation to you, who at the cost of the blood of His Son has opened a way for you into the Holiest, who waits in love to receive you again into His dwelling place as His child. Oh! I beseech you, *"let us* [all] *draw near."* Jesus Christ, the *"high priest over the house of God,"* is a perfect Savior.

"Let us draw near." The invitation comes especially to all believers. Do not be satisfied to stand outside the sanctuary. It is not sufficient to cherish the hope that your sins are forgiven. *"Let us draw near";* let us enter within the veil; let us, in spirit, press on into real nearness to our God. *"Let us draw near"* and live nearer to God, wholly taking up our abode in His holy presence. *"Let us draw near";* our place is the innermost sanctuary.

Let us, in spirit, press on into real nearness to our God.

"Let us draw near with a true heart in full assurance of faith." He who gives himself sincerely and entirely to God will, through the Holy Spirit, experience the *"full assurance of faith"* to take for himself, freely and gladly, all that the Word has promised. Our weakness of faith arises from duplicity of heart. *"Let us draw near with a true heart in full assurance"* that the blessing is ours. The blood has so perfectly atoned for and conquered sin that nothing can hold the believer back from free admission to God.

"Let us draw near…, having our hearts sprinkled from an evil conscience, and our bodies washed with pure

Dwelling in *The Holiest* through the Blood

water." Let us receive into our hearts faith in the perfect power of the blood, and let us lay aside everything that is not in accord with the purity of the Holy Place. Then we will begin to feel ourselves daily more at home in the Holiest. In Christ, who is our Life, we are also there. Then we will learn to carry on all our work in the Holiest. All that we do is a spiritual sacrifice well-pleasing to God in Jesus Christ. Dear brothers and sisters, *"let us draw near"* as God waits for us in the Holiest.

"Let us draw near." This call has special reference to prayer. Not as though we, as priests, are not always in the Holiest; but there are moments of closer fellowship when the soul turns itself entirely to God to be engaged with Him alone. Unfortunately, our prayer is too often a calling out to God from a distance, with little power in it. Let us, with each prayer, see that we are really in the Holiest. Let us, with hearts perfectly sprinkled from an evil conscience, in silent faith, take hold of the full effect of the blood, by which sin, as a separation between God and us, is entirely removed. Let us take time until we know, "I am in the Holiest through the blood," and then pray. Then we can lay our desires and wishes before our Father in the assurance that they are acceptable incense. Then prayer is a true drawing near to God, an exercise of inner fellowship with Him. Then we have courage and power to carry on our work of priestly intercession and to pray blessings on others. He who dwells in the Holy Place through the power of the blood is truly one of God's saints, and the power of God's holy and blessed presence goes out from him upon those who are around him.

The Power of the Blood of Christ

Brothers and sisters, *"let us draw near."* Let us pray for ourselves, for one another, for everyone. Let the Holiest so become our fixed abode that we may carry with us everywhere the presence of our God. Let this be the fountain of life for us that grows *"from strength to strength"* (Psalm 84:7), *"from glory to glory"* (2 Corinthians 3:18), always dwelling in the Holiest by the blood. Amen.

---

eight
Life in the Blood

---

eight

Life in the Blood

*Then Jesus said unto them, Verily, verily, I say unto you, Except
ye eat the flesh of the Son of man, and drink his blood, ye have
no life in you. Whoso eateth my flesh, and drinketh my blood,
hath eternal life; and I will raise him up at the last day. For my
flesh is meat indeed, and my blood is drink indeed. He that
eateth my flesh, and drinketh my blood,
dwelleth in me, and I in him.*
—John 6:53–56

*The cup of blessing which we bless, is it not
the communion of the blood of Christ?*
—1 Corinthians 10:16

The drinking of the blood of the Lord Jesus is the subject brought before us in these words. Just as water
has a twofold effect, so is it also with this holy blood.

When water is used for washing, it cleanses; but if we
drink it, we are refreshed and revived. He who desires to
know the full power of the blood of Jesus must be taught
by Him what the blessing of drinking the blood is. Everyone
knows the difference between washing and drinking. Necessary and pleasant as it is to use water for cleansing, it is

much more necessary and reviving to drink it. Without its cleansing, it is not possible to live as we ought; but without drinking, we cannot live at all. It is only by drinking that we enjoy the full benefit of its power to sustain life.

Without drinking the blood of the Son of God—that is, without taking hold of it heartily—eternal life cannot be obtained.

To many there is something unpleasant in the phrase "drinking the blood of the Son of Man," but it was still more disagreeable to the Jews, for the use of blood was forbidden by the Law of Moses under severe penalties. When Jesus spoke of drinking His blood, it naturally annoyed them, but it was also an unspeakable offense to their religious feelings. Our Lord, we may be sure, would not have used the phrase had He been able in some other way to make plain to them and to us the deepest and most glorious truths concerning salvation by the blood.

In seeking to become partakers of the salvation here spoken of as "drinking the blood of our Lord," let us endeavor to understand the following:

- First, what the blessing is that is described as "drinking the blood"
- Second, how this blessing is worked out in us
- Last, what our attitude should be toward it

The Blessing of "Drinking the Blood"

We saw just now that drinking expresses a much more intimate connection with water than washing and hence produces a more powerful effect. There is a blessing in the fellowship with the blood of Jesus that goes much further than cleansing or sanctification; rather, we are enabled to see how far-reaching the influence of the blessing indicated by this phrase is.

Not only must the blood do something for us, by placing us in a new relationship to God, but it must also do something in us, entirely renewing us within. The Lord Jesus drew our attention to this with these words: *"Except ye eat the flesh of the Son of man, and drink his blood, ye have no life in you."* Our Lord distinguished between two kinds of life. The Jews there in His presence had a natural life of body and soul. Many among them were devout, well-intentioned men, but He said they had no life in them unless they ate His flesh and drank His blood. They needed another life—a new, heavenly life that He possessed and that He could impart. All creaturely life must obtain nourishment outside of itself. The natural life was naturally nourished by bread and water. The heavenly life must be nourished by heavenly food and drink by Jesus Himself. *"Except ye eat the flesh of the Son of man, and drink his blood, ye have no life in you."* Nothing less must become ours than His life—the life that He, as Son of Man, lived on earth.

The heavenly life must be nourished by heavenly food and drink by Jesus Himself.

Our Lord emphasized this still more strongly when He again explained what the nature of that life is: *"Whoso eateth my flesh, and drinketh my blood, hath eternal life; and I will raise him up at the last day."* Eternal life is the life of God. Our Lord came to earth to reveal this eternal life in the flesh and then to communicate it to us who are in the flesh. In Him, we see the eternal life dwelling in its divine power, in a body of flesh, which was taken up into heaven. He told us that those who eat His flesh and drink His blood, who partake of His body as their sustenance, will also experience in their own bodies the power of eternal life. *"I will raise him up at the last day."* The marvel of the eternal life in Christ is that it was eternal life in a human body. We must be partakers of that body, no less than in the activities of His Spirit; then our bodies, also possessing that life, will one day be raised from the dead.

Earthly food is not real food, for it imparts no real life.

Our Lord said, *"My flesh is meat indeed, and my blood is drink indeed."* The word translated *"indeed"* here is the same as the one He used when He spoke His parable of the true vine: *"I am the true* [the indeed] *vine"* (John 15:1), thus indicating the difference between what was only a symbol and what is actual truth. Earthly food is not real food, for it imparts no real life. The one true food is the body and blood of the Lord Jesus Christ, which imparts and sustains life, and does so in no shadowy or merely symbolical manner. No, this Scripture indicates that, in a full and real sense, the flesh and blood of the Lord Jesus are the food by which eternal life is nourished and sustained in us: *"My flesh is meat indeed, and my blood is drink indeed."*

In order to point out the reality and power of this food, our Lord added, *"He that eateth my flesh, and drinketh my blood, dwelleth in me, and I in him."* Nourishment by His flesh and blood brings about the most perfect union with

Him. This is the reason that His flesh and blood have such power of eternal life. Our Lord declared here that those who believe in Him are to experience not only certain influences from Him in their hearts but are also to be brought into the closest and most abiding union with Him. *"He that...drinketh my blood, dwelleth in me, and I in him."*

This, then, is the blessing of drinking the blood of the Son of man: becoming one with Him, becoming a partaker of the divine nature in Him. How real this union is may be seen from the words that follow: *"As...I live by the Father: so he that eateth me, even he shall live by me"* (John 6:57). Nothing except the union that exists between our Lord and the Father can serve as a symbol of our union with Him. Just as in the indivisible, divine nature, the two Persons are truly One, so too does man become one with Jesus. The union is just as real as the one in the divine nature, only with this difference—that as human nature cannot exist apart from the body, this union also includes the body.

Our Lord prepared for Himself a body into which He took up a human body. This body became, by the body and blood of Jesus, a sharer in eternal life, in the life of our Lord Himself. Those who desire to receive the fullness of this blessing must be careful to enjoy all that the Scripture offers them in the holy mysterious expression, "to drink the blood of Christ."

How This Blessing Is Worked Out in Us

We will now try to understand what the "drinking of the blood of Jesus" really is.

The first idea that here presents itself is that "drinking" indicates the deep, true grasping in our spirits, by faith, of all we understand concerning the power of the blood.

We speak sometimes of "drinking in" the words of a speaker when we heartily give ourselves up to listen to and receive them. Likewise, when the heart of anyone is filled with a sense of the preciousness and power of the blood; when he, with real joy, is lost in the contemplation of it; when he, with wholehearted faith, takes it for himself and seeks to be convinced in his inner being of the life-giving power of that blood; then it may be rightly said that he "drinks the blood of Jesus." Everything that his faith enables him to see of redemption, of cleansing, of sanctification by the blood, he absorbs into the depths of his soul.

Drinking means a deep, true grasping in our spirits.

There is a deep truth in this representation, and it gives us a very glorious demonstration of the way in which the full blessing by the blood may be obtained. And yet it is certain that our Lord intended something more than this by so repeatedly making use of the expression about eating His flesh and drinking His blood. This further truth is becomes clear by His institution of the Lord's Supper. For, although our Savior did not actually deal with that Supper when He taught in Capernaum, He spoke on the subject of which later the Supper was made the visible confirmation.

In the Reformed churches, there are two aspects of viewing the Holy Supper. According to one view, which is that of the reformer Huldreich Zwingli (1484–1531), the bread and wine in the Supper are merely tokens, or representations of a spiritual truth to teach us that, as sure as bread and wine nourish and revive us when they are eaten or drunk, so surely—and even more surely—the body and blood recognized and taken hold of by faith nourish and quicken the soul.

According to the other view, put forth by John Calvin, there is something more than this in the eating of the Supper. He taught that, in a hidden and incomprehensible way, but no less truly, we, through the Holy Spirit, become so nourished by the body and blood of Jesus in heaven that even our bodies, through the power of His body, become partakers in the power of eternal life. Hence, he connected the resurrection of the body with the eating of Christ's body in the Supper. He wrote,

> The bodily presence which the Sacrament demands is such, and exercises such a power here (in the Supper) that it becomes not only the undoubted assurance in our spirit of eternal life, but also assures the immortality of the flesh. If anyone asks me how this can be, I am not ashamed to acknowledge that it is a mystery too high for my spirit to comprehend, or my words to express. I feel it more than I can understand it.

> It may seem incredible indeed that the flesh of Christ should reach us from such immense distance so as to become our food. But we must remember how far the power of the Holy Spirit transcends all our senses. Let faith then embrace what the understanding cannot grasp, namely: the sacred communication of His flesh and blood by which Christ transfuses His life into us, just as if it penetrated our bones and marrow.

Life in the Blood

The communion of the flesh and blood of Christ is necessary for all who desire to inherit eternal life. The apostle Paul said, *"The church...is his body"* (Ephesians 1:22–23); *"[Christ] is the head...from whom the whole body fitly joined together and compacted...maketh increase of the body"* (Ephesians 4:15–16). Our bodies are *"members of Christ"* (1 Corinthians 6:15). We see that all this cannot take place if He is not attached to us in body and spirit. The apostle again made use of a glorious expression, *"We are members of his body, of his flesh, and of his bones"* (Ephesians 5:30). Then he cried out, *"This is a great mystery"* (verse 32). It would therefore be foolish not to recognize the communion of believers in the body and blood of the Lord, a communion that the apostle esteemed so great that he wondered at it rather than explained it.

The communion of the flesh and blood of Christ is necessary for all who desire eternal life.

There is something more in the Supper than simply the believer taking hold of the redemptive work of Christ. This is made clear in the Heidelberg Catechism in Question 76: "What is it, then, to eat the crucified body of Christ and to drink His shed blood?" The answer is,

It is not only to embrace with a believing heart all the sufferings and death of Christ, and thereby to receive pardon of sin and eternal life; but also, besides that, to become more and more united to His sacred body by the Holy Spirit who dwells at once both in Christ and in us, so that we, though Christ is in heaven and we on earth, are, notwithstanding, flesh of His flesh, and bone of His bones; and we live and are governed forever by one Spirit.

The thoughts that are expressed in this teaching are in entire agreement with Scripture.

In the creation of man, the remarkable thing that distinguished him from the spirits that God had previously created and that made man the crowning work of God's wisdom and power was that he revealed the life of the spirit and the glory of God in a body formed out of dust. Through the body, lust and sin came into the world. Full redemption is designed to deliver the body and to make it God's abode. Redemption will be perfect and God's purpose accomplished only then. This was the purpose for which the Lord Jesus came in the flesh, and in Him dwelt *"all the fulness of the Godhead bodily"* (Colossians 2:9). For this, He *"bare our sins in His own body on the tree"* (1 Peter 2:24); and by His death and resurrection, He delivered the body, as well as the spirit, from the power of sin and death.

As the firstfruits of this redemption, we are now one body, as well as one spirit, with Him. We are of His body, of His flesh, and of His bones. Because of this, in the observance of the Holy Supper, the Lord comes to the body also and takes possession of it. He does not work by His Spirit only on our spirits, so that our bodies will one day share in redemption at the resurrection but do not share in it now. Rather, the body that is here on earth is the temple of the Spirit; and the sanctification of soul

Life in the Blood

and spirit will progress the more gloriously, to the extent that the undivided personality, including the body, which exercises such an opposing influence, has a share in it.

Thus we are in the Supper so intentionally fed by "the real natural body, and the real blood of Christ"*—not following the teaching of Luther that the body of Christ is so in the bread that even an unbeliever eats the holy body of Christ, but "real" in such a way that faith, in a secret way and by the Spirit, truly receives the power of the holy body and blood from heaven as the food by which soul and body become partakers of eternal life.

As the firstfruits of redemption, we are now one body and one spirit with Christ.

All that has now been said about the Supper must have its full application to the drinking of the blood of Jesus. It is a deep spiritual mystery in which the most intimate, the most perfect union with Christ, is brought about. It takes place where the soul, through the Holy Spirit, fully takes hold of the communion of the blood of Christ and becomes a true partaker of the disposition that He revealed in the shedding of His blood. The blood is the soul, the life of the body; where the believer, as one

---

* The words within quotation marks, "the real natural body, and the real blood of Christ," are quoted by Dr. Murray from the Articles of the Confession of Faith of the Reformed churches of Holland. Dr. Murray did not include the words immediately following, which declare that "the manner of our partaking of the same is not by the mouth, but by the Spirit, through faith." Dr. Murray remained true to the Reformed faith. His own view is expressed in his earlier quotation from the Heidelberg Catechism.

body with Christ, desires to abide perfectly in Him, there, through the Spirit and in a superhuman powerful way, the blood will support and strengthen the heavenly life. The life that was poured out in the blood becomes his life. The life of the old "I" dies to make room for the life of Christ in him. By perceiving how this drinking is the highest participation in the heavenly life of the Lord, faith has one of its highest and most glorious offices.

Our Attitude toward This Drinking

Beloved, you have already seen that we have here one of the deepest mysteries of the life of God in us. It is fitting that we draw near with very deep reverence while we ask the Lord Jesus to teach us and bestow upon us what He means by this drinking of His blood.

The life that was poured out in the blood becomes our life.

Only he who longs for full union with Jesus will truly learn what it is to drink the blood of Jesus. *"He that...drinketh my blood, dwelleth in me, and I in him."* He who is satisfied with just the forgiveness of his sins; he who does not thirst to drink abundantly of the love of Jesus; he who does not desire to experience redemption for soul and body, in its full power, so as to have truly in himself the same disposition that was in Jesus—he will have only a small share in this drinking of the blood. On the other hand, he who sets before him as his chief objective that which is also the objective of Jesus—*"Abide in me, and I in you"* (John 15:4)—and who desires the power of eternal life to operate in his body, he will not allow himself to be frightened by the impression that these words are too high or too mysterious. He longs to become heavenly minded because he belongs to heaven and is going there; therefore, he desires to obtain his food and drink from heaven. Without thirst, there is no drinking. The longing for Jesus and perfect fellowship with Him is the thirst that is the best preparation for being made to drink the blood.

It is by the Holy Spirit that the thirsty soul will be made to drink of the heavenly refreshment of this life-giving drink. We have already seen that this drinking is a heavenly mystery. In heaven where *"God the Judge of all"* (Hebrews 12:23) is, and where *"Jesus the mediator of the new covenant"* (verse 24) is, there is also *"the blood of sprinkling"* (verse 24). When the Holy Spirit teaches us—taking us, as it were, by the hand—He bestows more than our merely human understanding can grasp. All the thoughts that we can entertain about the blood or the life of Jesus, about our share in that blood as members of His body, and about the impartation to us of the living power of that blood, are only feeble rays of the glorious reality that He, the Holy Spirit, will bring into being in us through our union with Jesus.

Where, in our human bodies, do we find that the blood is actually received and, as it were, drunk in? Is it not through the veins, the bloodstream that is continually renewed from the heart? Each part of a healthy body ceaselessly and abundantly drinks in the blood. In the same way, the Spirit of life in Christ Jesus, who unites us to Him, will make this drinking of the blood the natural action of the inner life. When the Jews complained that what the Lord had spoken concerning eating His flesh and drinking His blood was *"an hard saying"* (John 6:60), He said, *"It is the spirit that quickeneth; the flesh profiteth nothing"* (verse 63). It is the Holy Spirit who makes this divine mystery life and power in us—a true living experience, in which we abide in Jesus and He in us.

On our part, there must be a quiet, strong, settled expectancy of faith that this blessing will be bestowed on us. We must believe that everything the precious blood can do or bestow is really for us.

Let us believe that the Savior Himself will cause us, through the Holy Spirit, to drink His blood unto life. Let us believe, and very heartily and continuously take hold of, those effects of the blood that we understand better: namely, its reconciling, cleansing, sanctifying effects.

We may then, with the greatest certainty and joy, say to the Lord, "O Lord, Your blood is my life-drink. You who have washed and cleansed me by that blood, You will teach me every day to *'eat the flesh of the Son of man, and drink his blood,'* so that I may abide in You and You in me." He will surely do this.

nine
Victory through
the Blood

nine

Victory through the Blood

*And they overcame him by the blood of the Lamb, and
by the word of their testimony; and they
loved not their lives unto the death.*
—Revelation 12:11

For thousands of years, there had been a mighty conflict for the possession of mankind, between the old Serpent, who led man astray, and "the seed of the woman." Often it seemed as though the kingdom of God had come in power; then, at other times, the might of evil obtained such supremacy that the battle appeared to be hopeless.

It was the same in the life of our Lord Jesus. By His coming and His wonderful words and works, the most glorious expectations of a speedy redemption were awakened. How terrible was the disappointment that the death of Jesus brought to all who had believed in Him! It seemed, indeed, as if the powers of darkness had conquered and had established their kingdom forever.

But, behold! Jesus is risen from the dead; an apparent victory proved to be the terrible downfall of the Prince of

Darkness. By bringing about the death of the Lord of life, Satan permitted Him, who alone was able to break open the gates of death, to enter his kingdom. *"Through death he...destroy[ed] him that had the power of death, that is, the devil"* (Hebrews 2:14). In that holy moment when our Lord shed His blood in death, and it seemed as if Satan were victorious, the Adversary was robbed of the authority he had possessed until then.

Our text verse gives a very grand representation of these memorable events. The best commentators, notwithstanding differences in details of exposition, are united in thinking that we have here a vision of the casting out of Satan from heaven as a result of the ascension of Christ.

We read in Revelation 12,

She brought forth a man child, who...was caught up unto God, and to his throne....And there was war in heaven: Michael and his angels fought against the dragon; and the dragon fought and his angels, and prevailed not; neither was their place found any more in heaven. And the great dragon was cast out, that old serpent, called the Devil, and Satan, which deceiveth the whole world: he was cast out into the earth, and his angels were cast out with him.

(Revelation 12:5, 7–9)

Then follows the song from which our text verse is taken:

Now is come salvation, and strength, and the kingdom of our God, and the power of his Christ: for the accuser of our brethren is cast down, which accused them before our God day and night. And they overcame him by the blood of the Lamb, and by

the word of their testimony; and they loved not their
lives unto the death. Therefore rejoice, ye heavens,
and ye that dwell in them. (Revelation 12:10–12)

The point that deserves our special attention is that, while the conquest of Satan and his being cast out of heaven are first represented as the results of the ascension of Jesus and the war in heaven that followed, yet in the song of triumph that was heard in heaven, victory is ascribed chiefly to the blood of the Lamb. The blood was the power by which the victory was gained.

Behold! Jesus is risen from the dead.

Throughout the book of Revelation, we see the Lamb on the throne. It is as the slain Lamb that He has gained that position: The victory over Satan and all his authority is by the blood of the Lamb.

I have spoken about the blood in its manifold effects. Now it is fitting that we seek to understand how victory is always ascribed to the blood of the Lamb. We shall consider the following:

- First, victory as gained once for all
- Second, victory as being always carried on
- Third, victory as something in which we have a share

The Victory That Was Gained Once for All

In the exalted representation given in our text, we see what a high position was once occupied by Satan, the great Enemy of the human race. He had entrance into heaven and appeared there as *"the accuser of our brethren"* (Revelation 12:10) and as the opponent of whatever was done in the interests of God's people.

The victory over Satan is by the blood of the Lamb.

We know how this is taught in the Old Testament. In the book of Job, we see Satan coming with the sons of God to present himself before the Lord and to obtain permission from Him to tempt His servant Job. (See Job 2.) We also read that Zechariah saw *"Joshua the high priest standing before the angel of the LORD, and Satan standing at his right hand to resist him* [or, *"be his adversary,"* RV]*"* (Zecheriah 3:1). Then there is the statement of our Lord, recorded in Luke 10:18: *"I beheld Satan as lightning fall from heaven."* Later on, in His agony of soul, as He felt beforehand His approaching sufferings, He said, *"Now is the judgment of this world: now shall the prince of this world be cast out"* (John 12:31).

It may, at first thought, seem strange that the Scriptures represent Satan as being in heaven. But to understand this correctly, it is necessary to remember that heaven is not a small, circumscribed dwelling place where God and Satan had a relationship as neighbors. No, heaven is a limitless sphere, with many different divisions, filled with innumerable hosts of angels who carry out God's will in nature. Among them, Satan also still held a place. Then remember, he is not represented in Scripture to be the black, grisly figure in outward appearance as he is generally pictured but as *"an angel of light"* (2 Corinthians 11:14). He was a prince with many thousands of servants.

When he had brought about the fall of man and had also transferred the world to himself and became its prince, he had real authority over all that was in it. Man had been destined to be king of this world, for God has said, *"Have thou authority"* (Luke 19:17). When Satan had conquered man, he took his entire kingdom under his authority, and this authority was recognized by God. God, in His holy will, had ordained that, if man listened to Satan, he would suffer the consequences and become subject to his tyranny. God never in this matter used His power or exercised force but always took the way of law and right; and so Satan retained his authority until it was taken from him in a lawful manner.

This is the reason he could appear before God in heaven, as Accuser of the brethren and in opposition to them, for the four thousand years of the old covenant. He had obtained authority over all flesh, and only after he was conquered in flesh, as the sphere of his authority, could he be cast out forever, as Accuser, from the court of heaven.

So the Son of God also had to come in the flesh in order to fight and conquer Satan on his own ground.

Also, for this reason, our Lord, at the commencement of His public life and after His anointing, being thus openly recognized as the Son of God, was *"led up of the Spirit into the wilderness to be tempted of the devil"* (Matthew 4:1). Victory over Satan could be gained only after He had personally endured and resisted his temptations.

But even this victory was not sufficient. Christ came in order that *"through death he might destroy him that had the power of death, that is, the devil"* (Hebrews 2:14). The Devil had that power of death because of the law of God.

That law had installed him as jailer of its prisoners. Scripture says, *"The sting of death is sin; and the strength of sin is the law"* (1 Corinthians 15:56). Victory over and the casting out of Satan could not take place until the righteous demands of the law were perfectly fulfilled. The sinner had to be delivered from the power of the law before he could be delivered from the authority of Satan.

Jesus willingly gave Himself up to bear the punishment of sin.

It was through His death and the shedding of His blood that the Lord Jesus fulfilled the law's demands. Ceaselessly, the law had been declaring that *"the wages of sin is death"* (Romans 6:23) and *"the soul that sinneth, it shall die"* (Ezekiel 18:4). By the ministry of the temple, by the sacrifices with the shedding of blood and sprinkling of blood, the law had foretold, through types, that reconciliation and redemption could take place only by the shedding of blood. As our surety, the Son of God was born under the law. He obeyed it perfectly. He resisted the temptations of Satan to withdraw Himself from under its authority. He willingly gave Himself up to bear the punishment of sin. He gave no ear to the temptation of Satan to refuse the cup of suffering. When He shed His blood, He had devoted His whole life, to its very end, to the fulfilling of the law. When the law had been thus perfectly fulfilled, the authority of sin and Satan was brought to an end. Therefore, death could not hold Him. *"Through the blood of the everlasting covenant"* (Hebrews 13:20), God brought Him *"again from the dead"* (verse 20). So also, He entered heaven *"by*

The Power of the Blood of Christ

his own blood" (Hebrews 9:12) to make His reconciliation effective for us.

The text verse gives us a striking description of the glorious result of the appearing of our Lord in heaven. Concerning the woman, we read,

> *She brought forth a man child, who...was caught up unto God, and to his throne....And there was war in heaven: Michael and his angels fought against the dragon; and the dragon fought and his angels, and prevailed not; neither was their place found any more in heaven. And the great dragon was cast out, that old serpent, called the Devil, and Satan, which deceiveth the whole world: he was cast out into the earth, and his angels were cast out with him.*
>
> (Revelation 12:5, 7–9)

Then follows the song of victory in which the words of our text occur: *"They overcame him by the blood of the Lamb."*

In the book of Daniel, we read of a previous conflict between this Michael, who stood on the side of God's people Israel, and the opposing world powers. But only now can Satan be cast out, because of the blood of the Lamb. Reconciliation for sin and the fulfillment of the law have taken all his authority from him. The blood, as we have already seen, that had done such wonderful things in heaven with God in blotting out sin and bringing it to nothing, had a similar power over Satan. He now no longer has any right to accuse. *"Now is come salvation, and strength, and the kingdom of our God, and the power of his Christ: for the accuser of our brethren is cast down...And they overcame him by the blood of the Lamb"* (Revelation 12:10–11).

Victory as Being Always Carried On

There is a progressive victory that follows this first victory. Since Satan has been cast down to earth, the heavenly victory must now be carried out here. This is indicated in the words of the song of victory, *"They overcame him by the blood of the Lamb."* This was primarily spoken concerning *"our brethren"* (verse 10) mentioned, but it also refers to the victory of the angels. The victory in heaven and on earth progresses simultaneously, resting on the same ground. We know from the passage in Daniel already mentioned (Daniel 10:12–13) about the fellowship that exists between heaven and earth in carrying on the work of God. As soon as Daniel prayed, the angel became active, and the three weeks' conflict in the heavenlies was three weeks of prayer and fasting on earth. The conflict here on earth is the result of a conflict in the invisible region of the heavenlies. Michael and his angels, as well as the brethren on earth, gained the victory *"by the blood* of *the Lamb."*

The blood has power over Satan.

In the twelfth chapter of Revelation, we are clearly taught how the conflict was moved from heaven to earth. *"Woe to the inhabiters of the earth,"* exclaimed the voice in heaven,

> *for the devil is come down unto you, having great wrath, because he knoweth that he hath but a short time. And when the dragon saw that he was cast unto the earth, he persecuted the woman which brought forth the man child.* (verses 12–13)

The Power of the Blood of Christ

The woman signifies nothing else than the church of God, out of which Jesus was born. When the Devil could not harm Him any more, he persecuted His church. The disciples of our Lord and the church in the first three centuries experienced this. In the bloody persecutions in which hundreds of thousands of Christians perished as martyrs, Satan did his utmost to lead the church into apostasy or to root it out altogether. But in its full sense, the statement that *"they overcame him by the blood of the Lamb, and by the word of their testimony; and they loved not their lives unto the death"* applies to the martyrs.

After the centuries of persecution, centuries of rest and worldly prosperity came to the church. Satan had tried force in vain. By the favor of the world, he might have better success. As the church conformed to the world, everything became darker and darker until, in the Middle Ages, the Roman apostasy reached its climax. Nevertheless, during all these ages, there were not just a few who, in the midst of surrounding misery, fought the *"fight of faith"* (1 Timothy 6:12) and, by the piety of their lives and witness for the Lord, the statement was often established: *"They overcame him by the blood of the Lamb, and by the word of their testimony; and they loved not their lives unto the death."*

This was no less the secret power by which, through the blessed Reformation, the mighty authority that Satan had gained in the church was broken down. *"They overcame him by the blood of the Lamb."* It was the discovery, experience, and preaching of the glorious truth that we are *"justified freely by his grace through the redemption that is in Christ Jesus: whom God hath set forth to be a propitiation through faith"* (Romans 3:24–25) that gave to the Reformers such wonderful power and such a glorious victory.

Since the days of the Reformation, it is still apparent that, to the extent that the blood of the Lamb is gloried in it, the church is constantly inspired by a new life to obtain the victory over deadness or error. Yes, even in the midst of the wildest heathen, where the throne of Satan has been undisturbed for thousands of years, this is still the weapon by which its power must be destroyed. The preaching of "the blood of the cross" as the reconciliation for the sin the world and the ground of God's free, forgiving love is the power by which the most darkened heart is opened and softened, and, from being a dwelling place of Satan, is changed into a temple of the Most High.

Where the blood of the Lamb is sprinkled, God dwells.

What avails for the church is available for each Christian. In *"the blood of the Lamb,"* he always has victory. When the soul is convinced of the power that the blood has with God in heaven to bring about a perfect reconciliation by the blotting out of sin; to rob the Devil of his authority over us completely and forever; to work out in our hearts a full assurance of the favor of God; and to destroy the power of sin—this is when the soul lives in the power of the blood and the temptations of Satan cease to ensnare.

The Power of the Blood of Christ

Where the holy blood of the Lamb of God is sprinkled, there God dwells and Satan is put to flight. In heaven, on earth, and in our hearts, that word as the announcement of a progressive victory is valid: *"They overcame him by the blood of the Lamb."*

Our Share in This Victory

We also have a share in this victory if we are reckoned among those who have been cleansed *"by the blood of the Lamb."* To have the full enjoyment of this, we must pay attention to the following facts.

No Victory without Conflict

We must recognize that we dwell in an enemy's territory. What was revealed to the apostle in his heavenly vision must hold good in our daily lives. Satan has been cast down to the earth; he has great wrath because he has only *"a short time"* (Revelation 12:12). He cannot now reach the glorified Jesus but seeks to reach Him by attacking His people. We must live always under the holy consciousness that we are watched, every moment, by an enemy of unimaginable cunning and power who is unwearied in his endeavor to bring us entirely, or even partially—however little it may be—under his authority. He is literally *"the prince of this world"* (John 12:31). All that is in the world is ready to serve him, and he knows how to make use of it in his attempts to lead the church to be unfaithful to her Lord and to inspire her with his spirit, the spirit of the world.

Not only does he make use of temptations to what is commonly thought to be sin, but he also knows how to gain an entrance into our earthly activities and businesses— our daily bread and necessary money, our politics, our commercial associations, our literature and science, our knowledge, and all things—so that he may make all that is lawful in itself into a tool to forward his devilish deceptions.

The believer who desires to share in the victory over Satan *"by the blood* of the *Lamb"* must be a fighter. He must make the effort to understand the character of his enemy. He must allow himself to be taught by the Spirit through the Word what the secret cunning of Satan is, which is called in Scripture *"the depths of Satan"* (Revelation 2:24), by which he so often blinds and deceives men. He must know that this battle is not *"against flesh and blood, but against principalities, against powers, against the rulers of the darkness of this world, against spiritual wickedness in high places"* (Ephesians 6:12). He must devote himself, in every way and at all costs, to carry on the battle until death. Only then will he be able to join in the song of victory, *"They overcame him by the blood of the Lamb, and by the word of their testimony; and they loved not their lives unto the death."*

The believer who desires to share in victory over Satan must be a fighter.

Victory through Faith

"And this is the victory that overcometh the world, even our faith. Who is he that overcometh the world, but he that believeth that Jesus is the Son of God?" (1 John 5:4–5). *"Be of good cheer,"* said our Lord Jesus, *"I have overcome the world"* (John 16:33). Satan is an already conquered enemy.

He has nothing by right—absolutely nothing—to say to one who belongs to the Lord Jesus. By not believing, or by letting go of my hold on, the fact that I have a participation in the victory of Jesus, I may again give Satan an authority over me that he does not otherwise possess. But when I know, by a living faith, that I am one with the Lord Jesus, that the Lord Himself lives in me, and that He maintains and carries on in me the victory that He gained, then Satan has no power over me. Victory *"by the blood of the Lamb"* is the power of my life.

Only this faith can inspire courage and joy in the conflict. By thinking of the terrible power of the Enemy, of his never-sleeping watchfulness, of the way in which he has taken possession of everything on earth by which to tempt us, it might well be said—as some Christians think—that the battle is too severe, that it is not possible to live always under such tension, that life would be impossible. This is perfectly true if we, in our weakness, had to meet the Enemy or gain the victory by our own might. But that is not what we are called upon to do. Jesus is the Victor; we need only to have our souls filled with the heavenly vision of Satan being cast out of heaven by Jesus, filled with faith in the blood by which Jesus Himself conquered, and filled with faith that He Himself is with us to maintain the power and victory of His blood. Then we also *"are more than conquerors through him that loved us"* (Romans 8:37).

Victory in Fellowship with the Blood of the Lamb

Faith is not merely a thought of which I lay hold, a conviction that possesses me. Rather, it is a life. Faith brings the soul into direct contact with God and the unseen things of heaven, but above all, with the blood of Jesus. It is not possible to believe in victory over Satan by the blood unless I myself am brought entirely under its power.

Belief in the power of the blood awakens in me a desire for an experience of its power in myself; each experience of its power makes belief in victory more glorious.

Seek to enter more deeply into the perfect reconciliation with God that is yours. Live constantly exercising faith in the assurance that *"the blood...cleanseth us from all sin"* (1 John 1:7); yield yourself to be sanctified and brought near to God through the blood; let it be your life-giving nourishment and power. You will thus have an unbroken experience of victory over Satan and his temptations. He who walks with God as a consecrated priest will rule as a conquering king of Satan.

Jesus is the Victor.

Believers, our Lord Jesus, by His blood, has made us not only priests but also kings unto God, not only so that we may draw near to God in priestly purity and ministry, but also that, in kingly power, we may rule for God. A kingly spirit must inspire us, a kingly courage to rule over our enemies. The blood of the Lamb must increasingly be a token and seal, not only of reconciliation for all guilt but also of victory over all the power of sin.

The resurrection and ascension of Jesus and the casting out of Satan were the results of the shedding of

The Power of the Blood of Christ

His blood. In you, also, the sprinkling of the blood will open the way for the full enjoyment of resurrection with Jesus and of being seated with Him in the heavenly places. (See Ephesians 1:20.)

I once more, therefore, urge you to open your entire being to the incoming of the power of the blood of Jesus. Your life will become a continual observance of the resurrection and ascension of our Lord and a continual victory over all the powers of hell. Your heart, too, will constantly unite with the song of heaven,

> *Now is come salvation, and strength, and the kingdom of our God, and the power of his Christ: for the accuser of our brethren is cast down, which accused them before our God day and night. And they overcame him by the blood of the Lamb.*
>
> (Revelation 12:10–11)

ten
Heavenly Joy
through the Blood

t e n

Heavenly Joy through the Blood

*After this I beheld, and, lo, a great multitude, which no man
could number,....stood before the throne, and before the
Lamb,...and cried with a loud voice, saying,
Salvation to our God which sitteth upon the throne,
and unto the Lamb....These are they which came out
of great tribulation, and have washed their robes,
and made them white in the blood of the Lamb.*
—Revelation 7:9–10, 14

These words occur in the well-known vision of the great multitude in heavenly glory, *"which no man could number."* In his spirit, the apostle saw them standing before the throne of God and of the Lamb, clothed with long white robes and with palm branches in their hands; and they sang with a loud voice, *"Salvation to our God which sitteth upon the throne, and unto the Lamb."* All the angels answered this song by falling down on their faces before the throne to worship God and to offer eternal praise and glory to Him.

Then, one of the elders, pointing out the great multitude and the clothing that distinguished them, asked John the question, *"What are these which are arrayed in white robes? and whence came they?"* (Revelation 7:13). John replied, *"Sir, thou knowest"* (verse 14). Then the elder said,

> *These are they which came out of great tribulation, and have washed their robes, and made them white in the blood of the Lamb. Therefore are they before the throne of God, and serve him day and night in his temple.* (verses 14–15)

This explanation, given by one of the elders who stood around the throne, concerning the state of the redeemed in their heavenly glory, is of great value. It reveals to us the fact that, not only in this world of sin and strife is the blood of Jesus the one hope of the sinner, but also in heaven, when every enemy has been subdued, the precious blood of Christ will be recognized forever as the ground of our salvation. And we learn that the blood must exercise its power with God in heaven, and not only as long as sin has still to be dealt with here beneath. But throughout eternity, to the praise and glory of the blood, each one of the redeemed will bear the sign of how the blood has availed for him and that he owes his salvation entirely to it.

The blood of Jesus will be forever recognized as the ground of our salvation.

If we have a clear insight into this, we will better understand what a true and vital connection there is between the *"sprinkling of the blood"* (1 Peter 1:2) and the joys of heaven, and that a true intimate connection with the blood on earth will enable the believer while still on earth to share the joy and glory of heaven.

Joy in heaven through the blood is possible because the blood does the following:

- First, it bestows the right to a place in heaven

- Second, it makes us fit for the pleasures of heaven

- Last, it provides subject matter for the song of heaven

The Blood Bestows the Right to a Place in Heaven

It is clear that this is the leading thought in the text verse. In the question, *"What are these which are arrayed in white robes? and whence came they?"* (Revelation 7:13), the elder desired to awaken attention and inquiry as to who these favored persons really are who stand before the throne and before the Lamb with palm branches in their hands. And, as he himself gives the reply, we expect that he will surely mention what might be thought to be the most remarkable thing in their appearance. He replied to the question *"Whence came they?"* by saying that they *"came out of great tribulation."* To the question *"What are these?"* he replied that they *"have washed their robes, and made them white in the blood of the Lamb."*

This is the one thing to which, as their distinguishing mark, he drew attention. This alone gives them the right to the place that they occupy in glory. This becomes evident if we notice the words that immediately follow: *"Therefore are they before the throne of God, and serve him day and night in his temple: and he that sitteth on the throne shall dwell among them"* (Revelation 7:15). It is because of the blood that they are before the throne. They owe it to the blood of the Lamb that they occupy that place so high in glory. The blood gives the right to heaven.

Right to heaven! Can such a thing be spoken of in connection with a condemned sinner? Would it not be better to glory only in the mercy of God who, by free grace, admits a sinner to heaven, than to speak of a *right* to heaven? No! It would not be better, for then we would not understand the value of the blood or why it had to be shed. We would also entertain false ideas about both our sin and God's grace, and remain unfit for the full enjoyment of the glorious redemption that the Savior has accomplished for us.

The blood gives the right to heaven.

I have already spoken of the casting out of Satan from heaven and have shown from this incident that a holy God always acts according to law. Just as the Devil was not cast out except according to law, so the sinner cannot be admitted in any other way. The prophet said, *"Zion shall be redeemed with judgment, and her converts with righteousness"* (Isaiah 1:27). Paul told us that *"grace reign*[s] *through righteousness"* (Romans 5:21). This was the purpose for which God sent His Son into the world. Instead of being afraid that speaking of having a right to enter heaven might belittle grace, it will be seen that the highest glory of grace consists in bestowing that right.

This insight is sometimes missing from the church, where it might be most expected. Recently I asked a man, who spoke of the hope he had of going to heaven when he died, on what ground he based his hope. He was not by any means a careless man, nor did he trust his own righteousness, yet he replied, "Well, I think that I do my best to seek the Lord, and to do His will." When I told him that this was no ground on which to stand before the judgment seat of a holy God, he appealed to the mercy of God. When I told him again that he needed more than mercy, it was something new for him to hear that it was only the righteousness of God that could grant him entrance into heaven. It is to be feared that there are many who listen to the preaching of "justification by faith" but who have no idea that they cannot have a share in eternal blessedness except by being declared legally righteous.

Entirely different was the testimony of a certain lad who did not have the full use of his intellectual abilities but whose heart the Spirit of God had enlightened to understand the meaning of the crucifixion of Jesus. When on his deathbed, he was asked about his hope, and he indicated that there was a great book that contained a page on which his many sins had been written. Then with the finger of his right hand, he pointed to the palm of his left hand, indicating the print of the nail there. Taking, as it were, something from the pierced hand—he was thinking of the blood that marked it—he showed how all that was written on that page was now blotted out. The blood of the Lamb was the ground of his hope.

The blood of the Lamb gives the believing sinner a right to heaven. *"Behold the Lamb of God, which taketh away the sin of the world"* (John 1:29). By shedding His blood, He really bore the punishment of sin. He gave Himself up to death in our place. He gave His life as *"a ransom for many"* (Matthew 20:28). The punishment has been borne, and our Lord's blood has really been shed as a ransom and appears before the throne of God in heaven. Thus, the righteousness of God declares that the sinner's surety, Jesus Christ, has fulfilled all the requirements of the law, regarding both punishment and obedience, and God pronounces the sinner who believes in Christ to be righteous. Faith is just the recognition that Christ has really done everything for me, that God's declaration of righteousness is only His declaration that, according to the law, I have a claim to salvation. God's grace bestows on me the right to heaven. The blood of the Lamb is the evidence of this right. If I have been cleansed by that blood, I can meet death with full confidence: I have a right to heaven.

If I have been cleansed by the blood, I can meet death with full confidence.

You desire and hope to get to heaven. Listen, then, to the answer given to the question, "Who are they who will find a place before the throne of God?" They *"have washed their robes, and made them white in the blood of the Lamb."* That washing takes place, not in heaven and not at death but here during our life on earth. Do not deceive yourself with a hope of heaven if you have not been cleansed, really cleansed, by that precious blood. Do not dare to meet death without knowing that Jesus Himself has cleansed you by His blood.

The Blood Bestows the Fitness for Heaven

It is of little use for men to have a right to anything unless they are equipped to enjoy it. However costly the gift, it is of little use if the inner disposition necessary to enjoy it is lacking. To bestow the right to heaven on those who are not at the same time prepared for it would give them no pleasure, but would be in conflict with the perfection of all God's works.

The power of the blood of Jesus not only sets open the door of heaven for the sinner, but it also operates on him in such a divine way that, as he enters heaven, it will appear that he and the blessedness of heaven have been really fitted for each other.

What constitutes the blessedness of heaven, and what the disposition is that is fitted for it, we are told by words connected with our text:

Therefore are they before the throne of God, and serve him day and night in his temple: and he that sitteth on the throne shall dwell among them. They shall hunger no more, neither thirst any more; neither shall the sun light on them, nor any heat. For the Lamb which is in the midst of the throne shall feed them, and shall lead them unto living fountains of waters: and God shall wipe away all tears from their eyes. (Revelation 7:15–17)

Nearness to and fellowship with God and the Lamb constitute the blessedness of heaven. To be before the throne of God, to see His face, to serve Him *"day and night in His temple"* (verse 15), to be overshadowed by Him who sits upon the throne, to be fed and led by the Lamb—all these expressions point out how little the blessedness of heaven depends on anything else than on God and the Lamb. To see them, to have intimacy with them, to be acknowledged, loved, and cared for by them—that is blessedness.

What preparation is needed for having such relationship with God and the Lamb? It consists of two things: inner agreement in mind and will, and delight in His nearness and fellowship. Both are purchased by the blood.

Nearness to and fellowship with the Lamb constitute the blessedness of heaven.

Inner Agreement in Mind and Will

There can be no thought of fitness for heaven apart from oneness with God's will. How could two dwell together unless they agree (Amos 3:3)? And because God is the Holy One, the sinner must be cleansed from his sin and sanctified; otherwise he remains utterly unfit for what constitutes the happiness of heaven. *"Without* [holiness] *no man shall see the Lord"* (Hebrews 12:14). Man's entire nature must be renewed so that he may think, desire, will, and do what pleases God, not as a matter of mere obedience in keeping a commandment but from natural pleasure and because he cannot do or will otherwise. Holiness must become his nature.

Isn't this just what we have seen that the blood of the Lamb does? *"The blood of Jesus Christ his Son cleanseth us from all sin"* (1 John 1:7). Where reconciliation and pardon are applied by the Holy Spirit and are retained by a living faith, there the blood operates with a divine power, killing sinful lusts and desires. The blood exercises constantly a wonderful cleansing power. In the blood, the power of the death of Jesus operates; we died with Him to sin. Through a believing relationship with the blood, the power of the death of Jesus presses into the innermost parts of our hidden lives. The blood breaks the power of sin and cleanses us from all sin.

The blood also sanctifies. We have seen that cleansing is only one part of salvation—the taking away of sin. The blood does more than this; it takes possession of us for God and inwardly bestows the very same disposition that was in Jesus when He shed His blood. In shedding that blood, He sanctified Himself for us, so that we also would be sanctified by the truth. As we delight and lose ourselves in that holy blood, the power of entire surrender to God's will and glory, the power to sacrifice everything and to abide in God's love that inspired the Lord Jesus, is at work in us.

The blood sanctifies us for the emptying and surrender of ourselves so that God may take possession of us and fill us with Himself. This is true holiness: to be possessed by and filled with God. This is worked out by the blood of the Lamb, and so we are prepared here on earth to meet God in heaven with unspeakable joy.

Delight in His Nearness and Fellowship

In addition to having one will with God, fitness for heaven also consists of the desire and capacity for enjoying fellowship with God. In this, the blood bestows, here on earth, the true preparation for heaven. We have seen how the blood brings us near to God, leading to a priestlike approach. Yes, we have liberty, by the blood, to enter into the Holiest of God's presence and to make our dwelling place there. We have seen that God attaches to the blood such incomprehensible value that, where the blood is sprinkled, there is His throne of grace. When a heart places itself under the full operation of the blood, there God dwells and there His salvation is experienced. The blood makes possible the practice of fellowship with God, and also with the Lamb, the Lord Jesus Himself. Have we forgotten His word, *"He that eateth my flesh, and drinketh my blood, dwelleth in me, and I in him"* (John 6:56)? The full blessing of the power of the blood, in its highest effect, is full abiding union with Jesus. It is only our unbelief that separates the work from the person, and the blood from the Lord Jesus. It is He Himself who cleanses by His blood, who brings us near, and who causes us to drink. It is only through the blood that we are fitted for full fellowship with Jesus in heaven, just as with the Father.

True holiness is to be possessed with and filled by God.

You who are redeemed, here you can see what is needed to mold you for heaven, to make you, even here, heavenly minded. See that the blood, which always has a place at the throne of grace above, always manifests its power in your hearts. Then your lives will become an unbroken fellowship with God and the Lamb—the foretaste of life in eternal glory. Let the thought enter deeply into your souls: Here on earth, the blood already bestows in the heart the blessedness of heaven. The precious blood makes life on earth and life in heaven one.

The Blood Provides Subject Matter for the Song of Heaven

What I have said so far has been taken from what the elder stated about the redeemed. But how far is this their experience and testimony? Have we anything out of their own mouths concerning this? Yes, they themselves bear witness. In the song contained in our text, they were heard to cry with loud voice, *"Salvation belongs to our God who sits on the throne, and to the Lamb!"* It is as the slain Lamb that the Lord Jesus is in the midst of the throne, as a Lamb whose blood had been shed. As such, He is the object of the worship of the redeemed.

This appears still more clearly in the *"new song"* that they sing,

> *Thou art worthy to take the book, and to open the seals thereof: for thou wast slain, and hast redeemed us to God by thy blood out of every kindred, and tongue, and people, and nation; and hast made us unto our God kings and priests.* (Revelation 5:9–10)

It also appears in words somewhat different, used by the apostle in the beginning of the book, where he, under the impression of all that he had seen and heard in heaven concerning the place that the Lamb occupied, at the first mention of the name of the Lord Jesus, cried out,

> *Unto him that loved us, and washed us from our sins in his own blood, and hath made us kings and priests unto God and his Father; to him be glory and dominion for ever and ever. Amen.*
>
> (Revelation 1:5–6)

Without ceasing, the blood of the Lamb continues to be the power to awaken the saved to their song of joy and thanksgiving. This is because, in the death of the cross, the sacrifice took place in which He gave Himself for them and won them for Himself. Because the blood is the eternal seal of what He did and of the love that moved Him to do it, it remains also the inexhaustible, overflowing fountain of heavenly bliss.

Heavenly Joy through the Blood

So that we may better understand this, notice the expression, *"Him that loved us, and washed us from our sins in his own blood"* (Revelation 1:5). In all our consideration about the blood of Jesus, we have had until now no occasion intentionally to stop there. And of all the glorious things that the blood means, this is one of the most glorious: His blood is the sign, the measure, yes, the impartation of His love. Each application of His blood, each time that He causes the soul to experience its power, is a fresh outflowing of His wonderful love. The full experience of the power of the blood in eternity will be nothing else than the full revelation of how He gave Himself up for us, and how He gives Himself to us in a love as eternal, unending, and incomprehensible as God Himself.

The blood is the eternal seal of what Christ did.

"Him that loved us, and washed us from our sins in his own blood" (verse 5). This love is indeed incomprehensible. What has that love *not* moved Him to do? He gave Himself for us (Galatians 1:3–4; 2:20); He became sin for us (2 Corinthians 5:21); He was made a curse for us (Galatians 3:13). Who would dare to use such language; who could ever have dared to think such a thing if God had not revealed it to us by His Spirit? Who would dare to say that He really gave Himself up for us, not because it was laid upon Him to do so, but by the impulse of a love that really longed for us, so that we might forever be identified with Him?

Because it is such a divine wonder, we feel it so little. But blessed be the Lord, there is a time coming when we will feel it; when, under the ceaseless and immediate love-sharing of the heavenly life, we will be filled and satisfied with that love. Yes, praised be the Lord! Even here on earth, there is hope that, through a better knowledge of and a more perfect trust in the blood, the Spirit will more powerfully pour out *"the love of God...in our hearts"* (Romans 5:5). There is nothing to prevent our hearts from being filled with the love of the Lamb and our mouths from being filled with His praise here on earth by faith, as is done in heaven by sight. Each experience of the power of the blood will become increasingly an experience of the love of Jesus.

It has been said that it is not desirable to lay too much emphasis on the word *blood,* that it sounds coarse, and that the thought expressed by it can be conveyed in a way more in accordance with our modern ways of speaking or thinking. I must acknowledge that I do not share this view. I receive this word as coming not just from John but from the Lord Himself. I am deeply convinced that the word chosen by the Spirit of God, and by Him made living and filled with the power of the eternal life from which the song containing it comes to us, carries in itself a power of blessing beyond our understanding. Changing the expression into our way of thinking has all the imperfection of a human translation. He who desires to know and experience *"what the Spirit saith unto the churches"* (Revelation 2:7) will accept the word by faith as having come from heaven, as the word in which the joy and power of eternal life is enfolded in a most distinct manner. Those expressions, *"Thy blood"* (Revelation 5:9) and *"the blood of the Lamb"* (Revelation 7:14; 12:11), will make the Holiest, the place of God's glory, resound eternally with the joyful notes of the *"new song"* (Revelation 5:9).

Heavenly Joy through the Blood

Heavenly joy, through the blood of the Lamb, will be the portion of all here on earth who, with undivided heart, yield to its power; and of all above in heaven who have become worthy to take a place among the multitude around the throne.

My comrades in redemption, we have learned what those in heaven say and how they sing about the blood. Let us pray earnestly that these tidings may have the effect on us that our Lord intended. We have seen that to live a real heavenly life, it is necessary to abide in the full power of the blood. The blood bestows the right to enter heaven.

May the blood be all our glory, not only at the cross but also at the throne.

As the blood of reconciliation, it works out in the soul the full, living consciousness that belongs to those who are at home in heaven. It brings us truly into the Holiest, near to God. It makes us fit for heaven.

As the cleansing blood, it delivers us from the lust and power of sin, and preserves us in the fellowship of the light and life of the holy God. The blood inspires the song of praise in heaven. As the blood of the Lamb *"who loved* [us], *and gave himself for* [us]" (Galatians 2:20), it speaks not only of what He has done for us, but chiefly of Him who has done all. In the blood, we have the most perfect impartation of Himself. He who, by faith, gives himself up to fully experience what the blood is able to do will soon find an entrance into a life of happy singing, of praise and love, that only heaven itself can surpass.

The Power of the Blood of Christ

My comrades in redemption, this life is for you and me. May the blood be all our glory, not only at the cross with its awesome wonders but also at the throne. Let us plunge deep, and ever deeper, into the living fountain of blood of the Lamb. Let us open our hearts wide, and ever wider, for its operation. Let us firmly, and ever more firmly, believe in the ceaseless cleansing by which the great eternal Priest Himself will apply that blood to us. Let us pray with burning desire, and ever more desire, that nothing—yes, nothing—may be in our hearts that does not experience the power of the blood. Let us unite joyfully, and ever more joyfully, in the song of the great multitude, who know of nothing so glorious as this: *"Thou...hast redeemed us to God by thy blood"* (Revelation 5:9).

May our lives on earth become what they ought to be: one ceaseless song to *"him that loved us, and washed us from our sins in his own blood, and hath made us kings and priests unto God and his Father; to him be glory and dominion for ever and ever. Amen"* (Revelation 1:5–6).

About the Author
Andrew Murray

About the Author

Andrew Murray

Andrew Murray (1828–1917) was an amazingly prolific Christian writer. He lived and ministered as both a pastor and author in the towns and villages of South Africa. Some of Murray's earliest works were written as extensions of his pastoral work, to provide nurturance and guidance for Christians, whether young or old in the faith. Once books such as *Abide in Christ, Divine Healing,* and *With Christ in the School of Prayer* were written, Murray became widely known, and new books from his pen were awaited with great eagerness throughout the world.

He wrote to give daily practical help to many of the people in his congregation who lived out in the farming communities and could only come into town for church services on rare occasions. As he wrote these books of instruction, Murray adopted the practice of placing many of his more devotional books into thirty-one separate readings to correspond with the days of the month.

At the age of seventy-eight, Murray resigned from the pastorate and devoted most of his time to his manuscripts. He continued to write profusely, moving from one book to the next with an intensity of purpose and a zeal that few men of God have ever equaled. He often said of himself, rather humorously, that he was like a hen about to hatch an egg; he was restless and unhappy until he got the burden of the message off his mind.

During these later years, after hearing of pocket-sized paperbacks, Andrew Murray immediately began to write books to be published in that fashion. He thought it was a splendid way to have the teachings of the Christian life at your fingertips, where they could be carried around and read at any time of the day.

One source has said of Andrew Murray that his prolific style possesses the strength and eloquence that are born of deep earnestness and a sense of the solemnity of the issues of the Christian life. Nearly every page reveals an intensity of purpose and appeal that stirs men to the depths of their souls. Murray moves the emotions, searches the conscience, and reveals the sins and shortcomings of many of us with a love and hope born out of an intimate knowledge of the mercy and faithfulness of God.

For Andrew Murray, prayer was considered our personal home base from which we live our Christian lives and extend ourselves to others. During his later years, the vital necessity of unceasing prayer in the spiritual life came to the forefront of his teachings. It was then that he revealed the secret treasures of his heart concerning a life of persistent and believing prayer.

Countless people the world over have hailed Andrew Murray as their spiritual father and given credit for much of their Christian growth to the influence of his priceless devotional books.

Steps to Peace With God

1. God's Purpose: Peace and Life

God loves you and wants you to experience peace and life—abundant and eternal.

The Bible Says ...

"We have peace with God through our Lord Jesus Christ." *Romans 5:1, NIV*

"For God so loved the world that He gave His only begotten Son, that whoever believes in Him should not perish but have everlasting life." *John 3:16, NKJV*

"I have come that they may have life, and that they may have it more abundantly." *John 10:10, NKJV*

Since God planned for us to have peace and the abundant life right now, why are most people not having this experience?

2. Our Problem: Separation From God

God created us in His own image to have an abundant life. He did not make us as robots to automatically love and obey Him, but gave us a will and a freedom of choice.

We chose to disobey God and go our own willful way. We still make this choice today. This results in separation from God.

The Bible Says ...

"For all have sinned and fall short of the glory of God." *Romans 3:23, NIV*

"For the wages of sin is death, but the gift of God is eternal life in Christ Jesus our Lord." *Romans 6:23, NIV*

Our choice results in separation from God.

People (Sinful)   God (Holy)

Our Attempts

Through the ages, individuals have tried in many ways to bridge this gap ... without success ...

The Bible Says ...

"There is a way that seems right to a man, but in the end it leads to death."
Proverbs 14:12, NIV

"But your iniquities have separated you from your God; and your sins have hidden His face from you, so that He will not hear."
Isaiah 59:2, NKJV

There is only one remedy for this problem of separation.

3. God's Remedy: The Cross

Jesus Christ is the only answer to this problem. He died on the cross and rose from the grave, paying the penalty for our sin and bridging the gap between God and people.

The Bible Says ...

"For there is one God and one mediator between God and men, the man Christ Jesus."
1 Timothy 2:5, NIV

"For Christ also suffered once for sins, the just for the unjust, that He might bring us to God."
1 Peter 3:18, NKJV

"But God demonstrates His own love toward us, in that while we were still sinners, Christ died for us." *Romans 5:8, NKJV*

God has provided the only way ... we must make the choice ...

4. Our Response: Receive Christ

We must trust Jesus Christ and receive Him by personal invitation.

The Bible says ...

"Behold, I stand at the door and knock. If anyone hears My voice and opens the door, I will come in to him and dine with him, and he with Me." *Revelation 3:20, NKJV*

"But as many as received Him, to them He gave the right to become children of God, to those who believe in His name." *John 1:12, NKJV*

"If you confess with your mouth the Lord Jesus and believe in your heart that God has raised Him from the dead, you will be saved." *Romans 10:9, NKJV*

Are you here ... or here?

Is there any good reason why you cannot receive Jesus Christ right now?

How To Receive Christ:

1. Admit your need (say, "I am a sinner").
2. Be willing to turn from your sins (repent) and ask for God's forgiveness.
3. Believe that Jesus Christ died for you on the cross and rose from the grave.
4. Through prayer, invite Jesus Christ to come in and control your life through the Holy Spirit (receive Jesus as Lord and Savior).

What To Pray:

Dear Lord Jesus,
    I know that I am a sinner, and I ask for Your forgiveness. I believe You died for my sins and rose from the dead. I turn from my sins and invite You to come into my heart and life. I want to trust and follow You as my Lord and Savior.

In Your Name, Amen.

_____   _____
Date   Signature

God's Assurance: His Word

If You Prayed This Prayer,

The Bible Says ...

"For, 'Everyone who calls on the name of the Lord will be saved.'"
Romans 10:13, NIV

Did you sincerely ask Jesus Christ to come into your life? Where is He right now? What has He given you?

"For it is by grace you have been saved, through faith—and this not from yourselves, it is the gift of God—not by works, so that no one can boast."
Ephesians 2:8–9, NIV

The Bible Says ...

"He who has the Son has life; he who does not have the Son of God does not have life. These things I have written to you who believe in the name of the Son of God, that you may know that you have eternal life, and that you may continue to believe in the name of the Son of God."
1 John 5:12–13, NKJV

Receiving Christ, we are born into God's family through the supernatural work of the Holy Spirit who indwells every believer. This is called regeneration or the "new birth."

This is just the beginning of a wonderful new life in Christ. To deepen this relationship you should:

1. Read your Bible every day to know Christ better.
2. Talk to God in prayer every day.
3. Tell others about Christ.
4. Worship, fellowship, and serve with other Christians in a church where Christ is preached.
5. As Christ's representative in a needy world, demonstrate your new life by your love and concern for others.

God bless you as you do.

Billy Graham

If you are committing your life to Christ, please let us know!
Billy Graham Evangelistic Association
1 Billy Graham Parkway, Charlotte, NC 28201-0001
1-877-2GRAHAM (1-877-247-2426)
billygraham.org